Praise for *Beautiful Tragedy*

"A beautiful succinctly written firsthand account of a mother losing her son and how faith and belief helped her deal with the grief.

"The author's anguish as a parent, as well as her family, clearly comes through in this book. I could almost feel the pain and grief and at points it was hard to continue reading.

"Written almost as a journal in the beginning, during, and aftermath of losing her son, the book packages in the main lessons, her taught principles that she put into place, and learned through this process.

"It's honest, transparent, very raw and it really draws you directly in to the situation as it's happening.

"This book from a mother's account will no doubt have you in floods of tears, but it also shows a real understanding of grief and loss. Anyone reading the book will be able to learn from her mantras, meditation and her principles. Her words are needed in today's conversation addressing the opioid epidemic.

"I feel the book will help give the necessary tools to those going through the grieving process, both the sincere notion of knowing they are not alone and how somebody who has felt their pain has been able to equip themselves with ways in which have helped them. I highly recommend this book!"

Glenn Marsden
CEO and founder of Imperfectly Perfect Campaign
www.imperfectlyperfectcampaign.org

"Judy writes with so much passion, authenticity, transparency, and courage. She is an inspiration to us all...this book is an amazing companion for those who are integrating the loss of a loved one into their lives. It can be read over and over again as one learns the practice of meditation and mindfulness to assist in the healing journey...I will absolutely be recommending this book to my clients in similar situations!"

Jennifer Cecil, M. Ed LPC
Licensed Professional Counselor
www.jennifercecil.org

"Judy has written an uplifting, easy-to-read guide to surviving the passing of a child that incorporates four cornerstones of self-care that she herself used when her son Jacob tragically passed. Through the G.I.V.E. principle: Grounding, Intention, Visualization and Expressing Gratitude, Judy gives us step-by-step instructions to leading a more purposeful and compassionate life, as well as to establishing a deeper connection with our loved ones in spirit. Judy and her beautiful son Jacob have given us proof that the love that we share with our children survives the death of the physical body."

Elizabeth Boisson
President and Co-Founder of Helping Parents Heal
www.helpingparentsheal.org

"Judy Thureson authentically and vulnerably delivers an inspiring and brave book that can help the masses with loss in a very warm and unique way. She allows us into her life and shows us how love can have no limits."

Kim Somers Egelsee
Author-Speaker-Life Coach
 # 1 bestselling author of Getting Your Life To a Ten+
www.kimlifecoach.com

"If you've ever experienced loss in your life, it is essential that you read Judy Thureson's, *Beautiful Tragedy.* She shares her story of tragically losing her young son. All told in such a raw, vulnerable, real and relatable way. She lets the reader into her heart; chronicling her anguish and leaving nothing to the imagination.

"Though her story is heart-wrenching, it is truly inspiring and uplifting. Judy's courage to stay present, honor her feelings and live in gratitude throughout this journey will be evident on every page. Judy also shares tools for staying mindful and grounded, even in your darkest moments.

"By the end, you will feel a new level of healing and more motivated to move forward and live your best life!"

Eden Sustin
Spiritual Medium, Host of Talk Purpose and Truth Podcast
www.edensustin.com

"Judy Thureson is an incredible woman with a unique and powerful story that transcends the depths of tragedy and suffering to find beauty and inspiration.

"Judy not only gives vulnerable voice to the journey of loss, but also provides mindfulness and meditation tools for healing. *Beautiful Tragedy* is a must read for anyone navigating the storms of loss."

Sandi Derby
Level II Advanced Certified Grief Recovery Specialist®
GRM Professional Development Coach & Life Coach
www.sandiatmore.com

"Judy and Erik are our dearest friends. We used to joke that our children were interchangeable because all of our kids spent so much time at each other's houses. We watched Jacob grow up into a talented and thoughtful young man...and we continue to feel his absence even now.

"It has been incredibly painful to experience this with Judy and Erik as they navigate the worst nightmare of every parent...the death of a child. And yet, to see them respond with such humility and grace has been nothing short of awe-inspiring.

"Combining her experience in meditation with her skills as a GR specialist, Judy has written a book that is so raw, so full of hope…that it will stay with you long after the last page has been turned.

"Judy is simply the strongest person that I know. A kind, compassionate warrior whose heart to make a difference and help others brings to life the words of Thornton Wilder,

> "Without your wounds where would your power be? It is your melancholy that makes your low voice tremble into the hearts of men and women. The very angels themselves cannot persuade the wretched and blundering children on earth as can one human being broken on the wheels of living. In Love's service, only wounded soldiers can serve."
>
> *Daniel & Vicki Hagadorn*
> *Co-founders, Preparing Kids 4 Life*
> *www.PK4L.com*

"I crossed paths with Judy and Erik at our support group for Parents of Addicted Loved Ones. PAL is a curriculum and support based group to help parents navigate the tumultuous waters as they deal with an addicted child.

"Judy and Erik had already implemented many of the principals supported by PAL and were allowing their adult son Jacob to direct his own path and live life on his own terms. In turn, they were taking care of themselves while continuing to love and support Jacob as they continued to pray for a breakthrough in recovery.

"In these pages, Judy shares her heartfelt memories of her beautiful son with all of his unique qualities that shaped the man that he grew up to be. Judy also shares with her audience her passion for meditation and the important role it has played in her own journey through grief and loss.

"As the father of two adult sons with substance use disorder and having faced several overdoses, homelessness, incarceration and general despair that accompanies addicted behaviors, I recommend this book to any parent of an addicted loved one. Rather than allow the darkness of addiction to quiet her voice she has become a beacon with a transparent account of the life of her son and a comfort to all who will read her story."

Kim Humphrey
Director, Parents of Addicted Loved Ones
Palgroup.org

Mary, Thank you for your support! Judy

Beautiful Tragedy

How to Cultivate Strength and Resilience During Life's Greatest Challenges

Judy Thureson

AVIVA
PUBLISHING
New York

Beautiful Tragedy: How to cultivate strength and resilience during life's greatest challenges

Aviva Publishing
Lake Placid, NY
518-523-1320
www.avivapubs.com

Judy Thureson
www.judythureson.com
judy@judythureson.com

Every attempt has been made to source all quotes properly.

For additional copies or bulk purchases visit:
www.judythureson.com

Editors: Erin Macleod, Kelleigh Averil, Annie K. Preston
Formatting & Interior Layout: Daniel Hagadorn
Cover Design: Erik Thureson
Author Photo: Denise Marie

Cataloging-in-Publication Data is on file at the Library of Congress
ISBN: 978-1-890427-34-4

10 9 8 7 6 5 4 3 2 1

First Edition, 2020

Printed in United States of America

This book is dedicated to everyone who has a dream in their hearts but are too afraid or insecure to go after them. Do it now, do it messy, do it when you are scared to do it! Your story matters, and your voice is needed in this world.

Thank you, Jacob, for being my biggest inspiration. Your example of living authentically has given me the strength to live unapologetically and fearlessly. I love you forever!

I used to tell you…"don't die with your song still inside of you." You exemplified this so beautifully…and this is my song.

CONTENTS

FOREWORD

On November 6th of 2015, I awoke in a pile of glass next to my rental car. As I sat up and slowly regained my wits, I recognized the blue and red lights flashing from the multiple vehicles surrounding me.

Six months later, I learned that the efforts of the police were not what had saved me from the overdose. It was being forced to watch myself on a 52" television screen in a Yellowstone County Courtroom being dragged lifeless from my car.

What happens in the mind, heart, and soul of an addict, to experience such a traumatic event, yet still feel the need to get high? There is really no one who can answer this question. Not the addict...and not the family that is forced to watch them continue down the heartbreaking road of addiction.

For more than a decade now, deaths from drug overdoses have been increasing at an alarming rate. With the introduction of fentanyl to America (and the world), the "War On Drugs" continues to claim countless lives, talents, and gifts. This "war" is being lost with no end in sight because it's being fought against the wrong enemy. As Ephesians 6:12 NIV says, "For our struggle is not against flesh and blood, but against the rulers, against the authorities, against the powers of this dark world and against the spiritual forces of evil in the heavenly realms."

The pages of this book reveal the heart of a loving mother who found a way to battle through the absolute worst nightmare of every parent...losing a child. Using meditation techniques to go even deeper into her faith in God, Judy turned her deepest tragedy into a beautiful blessing for others.

There is no dramatic hunt for a drug dealer, no blaming the doctor, not even a moment of blaming the very one who inflicted all the pain. Instead, Judy chose to fight the war on drugs in the most powerful way it can be fought...through the practice of spiritual inner peace.

At times, you may feel tears coming to your eyes. It could be from a place of compassion for her loss, or perhaps from a place of understanding as she describes something you have experienced yourself. I can't encourage you enough to put into practice her meditation techniques in your own struggles for inner peace.

On November 6th, 2017, I put a mind-altering substance in my body for the last time. Five days later, I had a dramatic encounter with Jesus, who pulled me from the muck of homelessness and drug addiction through a series of miracles, signs, and wonders. I was truly one of the lucky ones. At the time of this writing, less than 10% of addicts like myself ever experience long-term recovery.

Two years later to the day, I launched my book *From Chains To Saved: One Man's Journey Through The Spiritual Realm of Addiction*. I had been afraid to share these things for so long because of what I thought people might think of me. But after publishing the book and receiving countless messages, emails, and in-person conversations, I realized there was something to this...and Recovered On Purpose was born.

At Recovered On Purpose, we believe that the stories of recovered addicts are the most powerful weapons against the invisible enemy in the war on drugs. We are raising an army of recovered addicts whose stories give hope for other addicts to find their own freedom. Their stories will be shared in schools across the country so that future generations can be detoured from going down the same path we did.

When Judy asked me to write the foreword to this book, I was incredibly honored to be part of a story that will contribute to the healing of those trapped in addiction. I have personally lost too many friends and loved ones to this epidemic. This book is a gift filled with a mother's love and with practical guidance for anyone going through a time like this. Thank you, Judy.

I remember watching that television screen, seeing my own body being dragged through glass and the emergency first responders desperately trying to save my life. My only thought was sadness for what I had been doing to myself. But I was totally ignorant of the pain I was causing my loved ones.

The night before beginning to read this book, I wrote down the intention to start a 15-minute per day morning meditation practice. I began that practice just an hour before opening these pages, and the significance of that will become clear in a moment.

It is my belief that this book came at the perfect time for both myself, and for the people I will be gifting it to. So, if you are reading these words, this book has come at the perfect time for you as well. Whether you are experiencing a season of crisis or a season of grief...inner peace will be your most valuable asset. The practices within are incredibly powerful and you are holding the exact book you were meant to have.

Abundant love & blessings to you,

Adam Vibe Gunton
Founder, Recovered On Purpose

Introduction

In June of 2019, I survived the traumatic loss of my beautiful son, Jacob, from an opioid overdose. What I have written are the words and tools that guided me through my deepest darkness.

My hope and prayer is that my story will help you on your grief journey or assist you as you walk alongside a loved one on theirs. This book is just a snapshot of my own journey.

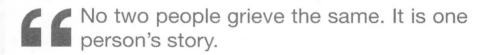

> No two people grieve the same. It is one person's story.

I hope my words will help free you and allow yourself to feel the pain and not second guess the emotions rushing through you. My steps to recovery might not be the same as yours and that's okay.

But if this helps give you some strength and structure for the days to come, then I am grateful I can help support you. Be gentle with yourself. Sometimes it just feels good to know you are not alone on your journey.

If you are grieving the loss of a loved one, this book is for you. I wrote this book thinking about you, your pain, your broken heart, and I didn't want you to be alone. I want you to know how sorry I am for your loss. I want you to know that I see you, I feel your pain, and I am right here with you.

Cultivating strength and resilience is not reserved for the strong on the contrary your greatest strength will come out of your greatest weakness. Doing the next right thing no matter how big or how small is the secret to overcoming this painful season.

My vision for you is to read this book from start to finish. As you read my thoughts each day, I want you to use the structure of the mindfulness and meditative techniques that I call the **G.I.V.E. Principle** on your own journey.

If you have never meditated before, don't worry. There is no right or wrong way to meditate. You can go to my website, **www.judythureson.com**, to learn more and do a guided meditation with me. Sometimes it helps to have a visual.

I have meditated on and off for almost thirty years! But over the last year, I have developed a daily discipline that has changed my life. This was the missing link for me. If we take care of our bodies through diet and exercise, but we neglect our emotional, spiritual, and mental health, then we are not living up to our full potential.

What good is it to eat organic, go to the gym, and drink filtered water, yet do nothing when our minds are toxic!? What I am suggesting will only take fifteen minutes a day to start.

Once you've developed a rhythm and a consistent schedule, you can add another fifteen-minute session in the afternoon or evening. Trust me, once you get the hang of it, you'll be looking forward to this sacred time for yourself. Commit to a time and place and try it.

You will be amazed at the benefits this practice will have on your well-being.

You don't have to have a perfect Zen space to meditate. You can do this anywhere. It doesn't have to be quiet and tranquil, either. Let's get real, the moments you need meditation the most are when you are in the middle of chaos!

However, it would be beneficial to find a location where you can sit comfortably with your back supported and you are able to close your eyes. I know I don't have to sell you on meditation.

There are so many studies and statistics of its numerous benefits. The research that validates the importance of mindfulness and meditation are astounding! This is just my version of meditating through grief.

There are four sections to my practice. This is what I call the **G.I.V.E. Principle**.

In the midst of deep grief and trauma, the last thing I want to do is take care of myself. I can't eat, sleep, or think…let alone breathe. I made a conscious decision to give nourishment to myself *first* with the **G.I.V.E. Principle**.

I realize that I cannot pour from an empty cup, I have to pour into *me* first and give out of my overflow; otherwise, I will be left feeling empty and burned out. This is the greatest gift I can give myself during this harrowing time.

When you are on a plane and a flight attendant gives you direction, in case of emergency, you put the oxygen mask on yourself first, then help the person next to you. This is the same idea. We must give to ourselves first. Self-care is not selfish. It is vital!

With this practice, I was able to be fully present and experience all that was happening around me. We must be willing to feel everything and not be afraid of the pain. Running away from it won't change the facts.

Every day we were in the hospital with Jacob was a gift. My tendency would have been to feel anxious and worried, but with this practice I was able to ground myself and savor every last moment with my son.

Grounding: Mindfulness, according to Jon-Kabat-Zinn, the founder of the Mindfulness-Based Stress Reduction (MBSR) practice, is "the awareness that arises through paying attention, on purpose, in the present moment non-judgmentally."

Merriam Webster's definition is "the practice of maintaining a non-judgmental state or heightened or complete awareness of one's thoughts, emotions, or experiences on a moment-to-moment basis."

During the mindfulness section of our daily practice, it's important to be self-aware. Self-awareness is the ability to have a clear perception and/or understanding of oneself. This includes strengths, weaknesses, thoughts, beliefs, and emotions.

Grounding will help you to connect your breath to all five senses: sight, smell, hearing, taste, and touch; grounding yourself with every session. Grounding is an essential part of the grieving process. The grounding practice will teach you how to live in the NOW!

Intention: Meditation mantra - The definition of the word "mantra" simply means mind vehicle. You are taking a chosen word, your intention, phrase, or affirmation, deep inside your mind, body, and spirit.

This is a powerful tool that some experts claim can help release stress and trauma from the body. We are actually disciplining our mind to get out of anxious thinking. This will help you to be intentional about calming the body and soul.

Think of this as your daily workout for your brain. I've also heard someone describe it as your mind going to the bathroom. This is the time where you will release all the mental toxic waste from your mind, body, and spirit.

This part of the practice helps you to re-wire old thought patterns and negative belief systems, while assisting you in creating new positive thought patterns and new pathways. This is all done to make room for brand new thoughts and ideas. Intentions help us to change our PAST patterns.

Visualization: This technique allows you to exercise your faith. Faith is defined as believing in something you cannot see. This is where we imagine and envision a better scenario than the one we are currently in. This is where we manifest our dreams and desires and speak them into existence!

Our emotions drive our actions. Imagine and visualize what it feels like to be in the new perceived state. Our belief and behavior must begin with what we can visualize and imagine. This practice helps our minds focus on an abundance mindset versus a scarcity mindset.

Visualization keeps our hearts and minds open to positive possibilities. Visualization prepares us for the FUTURE.

Expressing Gratitude: It is critical to end each practice with gratitude. Our perspective and viewpoint are the most important parts of how we are going to respond to the world around us. No matter how bleak things may seem, there will always be reasons to be grateful. You will always have a choice.

It has been proven that high levels of stress keep your brain limited to the problem. Gratitude expands your mind to see abundance and hope. I encourage you to not just choose gratitude, but to express gratitude. Saying it out loud and the act of encouraging those around you will truly change your life. Science supports the idea that gratitude re-wires the brain and elevates your mood.

Expressing gratitude is the ACTION part of this practice.

The optimal way to practice this is to do all four parts together. You can certainly use these tools separately. There might be days where you'll spend more time on grounding, or gratitude; that's okay. Give yourself permission to connect to what you need. Generally, it should be broken down like this:

- **G** rounding (4 minutes)
- **I** ntention (7 minutes)
- **V** isualization (2 minutes)
- **E** xpressing Gratitude (2 minutes)

It will take practice and patience to begin a new discipline like this. If you are not used to it, it can feel uncomfortable, your mind may race, and you might feel silly. It's okay. Be patient with yourself. Keep practicing.

Trust yourself. Trust your spirit. Trust your higher power.

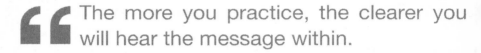 The more you practice, the clearer you will hear the message within.

Call it whatever you are comfortable with. Spirit guide, Holy Spirit, intuition, gut instinct, little small voice, sixth sense, God, whatever you call it, we all have it. It is a sense of knowing.

You can't put your finger on it. Yet, it is a feeling you cannot deny. The more you practice, the clearer you will hear the message within. Also feel free to incorporate your faith into this practice.

As a Christian, I call the inner voice that I hear, God, or the Holy Spirit, and I use this practice as part of my prayer time.

I found this daily discipline essential to my grief process.

I want to suggest to you that you are already an expert

meditator and you don't even know it. Let me explain…

In times of stress and trauma, it is in our nature to respond in direct opposition to these four steps.

In essence, we are already doing these four steps, just in a way that is polar opposite to growth and healing.

For example, the opposite of **Grounding** is the tendency to escape, numb out, and/or disassociate. This is typically our default response during heightened anxiety.

Intention is when we tend to ruminate over the "what if's", past disappointments, mistakes, and shame. We focus on the negative self-talk that continues to take us on a downward spiral.

Visualization is when we tend to imagine the worst-case scenario rather than intentionally focusing on the results that we want to see happen.

Expressing Gratitude can end up as a way to focus on what we don't have, rather than what we do have.

I submit that we are already living these four steps daily, without intention, in a negative, destructive way. We simply need to flip it and take action to intentionally set our mind to this disciplined way of thinking. Any time we have an opportunity to get out of auto-pilot mode, we should. Our default is often negative. We have the power to choose something different every day.

Start today.

I challenge you to join me on this journey. Consistency is critical; being consistent in this practice is key to making a positive change. Track your progress every day as you begin to identify the areas where you feel less anxious and more hopeful.

For example, record these four things and track your progress:
On a scale of 1 to 10, with 10 being the best, how is your...

Chronic Pain (scale of 1 to 10 with 10 being highest) Where is your pain? Headaches? Stomach aches? Stiffness? Bloating?

Beginning Date: _____ / _____ / _____ Scale of 1-10: _____

Ending Date: _____ / _____ / _____ Scale of 1-10: _____

Attitude (scale of 1 to 10 with 10 being best) How are your emotional outbursts? Anger? Sadness? Irritability?

Beginning Date: _____ / _____ / _____ Scale of 1-10: _____

Ending Date: _____ / _____ / _____ Scale of 1-10: _____

Stress (scale of 1 to 10 with 10 being highest)

Beginning Date: _____ / _____ / _____ Scale of 1-10: _____

Ending Date: _____ / _____ / _____ Scale of 1-10: _____

Sleep (scale of 1 to 10 with 10 being best) How many hours are you sleeping? Is it restless/restful? Interrupted?

Beginning Date: _____ / _____ / _____ Scale of 1-10: _____

Ending Date: _____ / _____ / _____ Scale of 1-10: _____

At the end of faithfully tracking your information for 40 days, what stands out most to you?

What have you learned about yourself while you try to endure your pain?

Remember, you first, then the rest of the world. Your family needs you; if you are not strong, you won't be able to help them.

The Backstory

On August 16, 2019 I woke up in the middle of the night to a voice in my dream giving me the title for this book, "Beautiful Tragedy." I wrote it down in my notes and went back to bed. I didn't really think about it.

On September 5, 2019 I had coffee with my friend, Kristyn Goold, and with tears in her eyes, she suggested that I write a book. She told me that she was impacted by my faith journey and that my story needed to be told.

Again, I listened but in my time of grief, honestly...writing a book was not high on my priority list.

On September 9, 2019, I was awakened in the middle of the night again! This time, I wasn't sure if I was asleep or dreaming. I heard a voice say, "You are a writer!"

Again, he said, "You are a writer!"

It wasn't an encouraging prompt, like, "Hey, you can do it!" It was more forthright and even sounded a bit annoyed. Like, "Stop making excuses and write this book!"

I began writing some notes on my phone and by 5:00AM on the morning of September 27th, the book was complete! What!? How is that even possible? Like eighteen days!?

Apparently, I had a lot to share and needed to get it out of my head and heart and onto paper.

Chapter 1 Be Still

"All I have is all I need and all I need
is all I have in this moment."

BYRON KATIE

The morning of June 13th began like any other day. My husband, Erik, and I had coffee and breakfast around 9:30 AM We were finalizing the last-minute details on a new meditation program I was launching. It was a 30-day video program that Erik was going to produce and shoot. I was crystal clear, and laser focused on what I was going to create. I was sitting at the dining room table and Erik was in the kitchen pouring himself a cup of coffee when I blurted out, "I feel apprehensive, because whenever I get close to doing something like this, something bad happens to Jacob."

Jacob is our eighteen-year old son who in the last couple of years was having challenges with his mental health and substance abuse.

You see, I lead a women's empowerment group with one of my best friends, Vicki. We hosted an amazing conference in 2017, and after the conference, we met with our husbands to talk about going all-in and really getting focused on our mission. Shortly after this commitment, we found out that Jacob, our 16-year-old son, was using drugs. We decided to put everything on the back burner so I could focus on helping him with his recovery.

The next couple of years were rough, to say the least. We found ourselves in and out of rehab, doctor appointments, therapy, battling Jacob's mental illness and addiction. His struggle with depression and anxiety had been the catalyst for his drug use. It was a challenging season, full of fear and anxiety.

After much work and commitment, we entered a peaceful season, with Jacob seemingly doing better. I decided, once again, to focus on our Get Inspired Movement and finish up a book Vicki and I had been working on.

No sooner had I made that commitment, that Jacob ended up in the ER once again for a drug overdose. Naturally, I put my work on hold and focused on Jacob's recovery. As his mom, Jacob's health and wellness was my number one priority. Our entire family was committed. We went to numerous doctors, therapists, and psychiatrists. We tried in-patient rehab, outpatient rehab, AA, NA, you name it, we did it.

So, as you can imagine, on June 13th, as I thought about undertaking this new project, I was a little on edge and hesitant. I was afraid to be this close to launching a new venture and having something bad happen to Jacob again. That's when Erik said, "Look at me. This time nothing is going to stop you from making this happen. Listen to me, not even Jacob. Jacob is not going to derail this. Do you understand me?"

I looked at him and nodded, but I was still anxious.

It wasn't too long after the conversation that I received a phone call from Jacob's girlfriend, Evelyn. She told me that she found Jacob unresponsive from an apparent drug overdose and that paramedics were on their way. As I've stated, sadly, this was not our first experience with Jacob being rushed to the ER, so I practiced how to better respond, surprisingly not completely losing it. I took deep breaths and used my mindfulness and meditation techniques to not go to the worst-case scenario.

Our family immediately packed up the car and drove to Los Angeles as soon as we heard the news. Maybe it was denial or self-preservation, yet, we were all calm and hopeful. We didn't have all the details yet and that prevented us from freaking out.

The next forty days chronicle what our journey looked like. Beginning on June 13th with the phone call, all the way to the aftermath of our tragic experience losing my one and only son, Jacob, to an opioid overdose.

I want to invite you to take a peek at what I was going through and how I processed daily. I can't believe that the meditation/mindfulness program that I was going to launch would become the very tools to get me through my 'dark night of the soul' experience.

In a weird way, Erik was right. Jacob did not derail my commitment and goal. If anything, Jacob propelled this program and book.

The six-hour drive was unusually normal. I think we were all in shock and to be honest, probably in denial. We had been in this situation before and didn't know if this was just another one of those stints. The mood in the car was tense, but not emotional.

Emma played DJ and skipped around her Soundcloud playlist to occupy her mind. I meditated, prayed, prayed some more, and talked myself into believing that everything was going to be okay. Erik was focused on the drive and Sydney was just happy to be going to Los Angeles for her summer vacation.

Sadly, the days to come were the farthest thing from a vacation.

G.I.V.E. Principle

Grounding

I take a few breaths and bring awareness to my body. I breathe through my nose and check in with myself. I recognize my five senses. What I see (I name four things in the room). What I hear. What I smell. What I taste. What I feel with my sense of touch.

I take a moment to *be still*. I continue to take deep, conscious breaths. This is important to ground myself and be present.

I will demonstrate how to process the G.I.V.E. Principle, then you will try it. Whatever you are going through, I believe these mantras, and intentions will resonate with you. Feel free to apply it to your own life and journey.

Now you try it. Take a few breaths and bring awareness to your body. Breathe through your nose and check in with yourself. Recognize your five senses. What do you see? Name three to four things in the room. What do you hear? What do you smell? What do you taste? What do you feel with your sense of touch?

Take a moment to be still. Continue to take deep, conscious breaths.

This is important to ground yourself and be present.

Intention: Be still

Today's intention is to *be still*. It proves to be super important for the days to come.

 This intention is a constant reminder to *be still*, stay in the moment, and to not go to the dark places that are tempting me.

When those fears and thoughts start to creep into my mind, I immediately block them with the mantra, *be still*.

Now you try it. You are going to take this mantra and say it over and over to yourself as much as you need. Remember that this present moment is all that you need. You have zero control of what happened before or what is going to happen next. Begin by bringing your intention into your mind vehicle, your mantra.

Take this word: be still and bring it to the forefront of your mind. As you look within, notice what you are feeling. Are you being still? Is your heart racing? Are you anxious?

Begin to repeat the mantra over and over. Bring the intention down to your nose, inhale stillness, exhale anxiety.

As you listen to your surroundings, remember that you have the ability to tap into your inner peace. Whatever chaos is going on around you, you have the ability to shut it out and choose to only listen to what is positive. As you bring attention to your mouth, remember that your words contain the power of life and death.

Choose to speak life! Speak positivity. Continue to bring your word to your heart center. This is where we wrestle with the fears and anxiety of the unknown.

Choose to focus on the *right here, right now*.

Bring your intention to your core center, your vessel, your temple, your being; this is where the Holy Spirit resides, this is where you tap into the supernatural power of peace.

This peace is unfathomable and indescribable.

You won't even believe the stillness and peace you will experience when you go directly to the limitless source for the power. Now as we go deeper, we bring the word, our mantra, our intention, down to our reproductive area. This is where we give birth to hope and dreams.

How we show up here determines how we impact those around us. Our peace will be the barometer for how others will receive the peace we give. Our attitude will be contagious and spread to those around us.

As we continue to bring the word down to our feet, we are reminded that we all have a path, we are all on a journey, and we all have a destiny. Breathe in stillness and walk toward your destiny with peace. Exhale out anything and everything that you do not need here.

As you focus on your hands, remind yourself that they have the ability to build up, create, encourage, caress, and hold. As you imagine peace covering all of you, imagine a bright white light blanketing your entire body. Now, take all of that light and go all the way from the ground, back up to your head.

Visualization

I visualize Jacob waking up and not having any brain damage. I keep seeing him sitting up and smiling, wondering what happened. I cherish this picture in my heart and in my mind.

Today, my gratitude is simply, "I am grateful Jacob is in the ER and that our family can be here with him, feeling his warm body, kissing, hugging him, and being able to verbally tell him that we love him."

Now you try it. Take a moment to visualize what you want to see happen. What does the change you desire look like? Imagine peace in your heart, peace in your body language, peace in your speech, peace in every fiber of your being.

What does it look like? What is the picture you envision in your mind? What does it feel like? What does it smell like?

I want you to put yourself in this word picture and really feel what it is like to be there.

Express Gratitude

Take time to be grateful. This is the most important part of the practice. This will enable you to have a perspective change. Gratitude exposes the possibility that we can open our hearts to the best-case scenario. Gratitude literally changes our attitude.

Erik is the best example of expressing gratitude. He has this natural, compassionate, giving attitude, even in the midst of his own grief. I watch him connect to people all the time and I stand in awe. We can go anywhere, and he will find a new friend. He is such a great example of having an attitude of gratitude. He inspires me.

Now you try it. This is the action part of the program that truly makes a difference during your grieving process. The shift in our minds and hearts to gratitude changes the trajectory of our day.

Our focus changes and our hearts can experience a difference in the emotions that we feel from pain and sorrow to maybe a glimmer of hope and a glimpse of joy.

Find a person you can encourage and speak life to. Find a way to spread joy and light even in the midst of your own brokenness. That's how the light comes in.

Chapter 2 | I Will Fight For You

"The Lord will fight for you; you need only be still."

EXODUS 14:14 NIV

Today is Day Two, and it is a rough day. Jacob doesn't look like he has any fight left in him. I hang on to this mantra: No matter what happens, I will fight for my son. No matter what happens, God is fighting for me.

Jacob does not look good today. As soon as I walked into his hospital room, I felt hopeless. Looking at Jacob's shell of a body, I could not feel his spirit. Everything in the room felt vacant, distant, and cold. In my mind, I was wrestling with the idea that there was no coming back from this. This would be the end. I forced myself to take every thought captive and think faithful thoughts. I do not have the luxury to think about anything else. At this moment, I have to choose to believe and trust that God knows I am not ready to let go of Jacob. I cannot imagine my life without him. Please God, do not take him. Fight for me so I have the strength to fight for him, too. Give Jacob the strength. I am begging you.

This is the battle that I fight in my heart. I have to make a decision to trust and believe that it isn't over. We are not ready. As I begin to bring the intention closer to my core center, I tap into the supernatural power of the Holy Spirit. I know that this kind of faith and belief will have to come from God himself because I do not have it. I choose to believe. I choose to fight. I need to bring my strength and faith to the hospital, and I want to share it with all of those around us because we all need it.

G.I.V.E. Principle

Grounding

Begin by taking a few deep breaths. Be aware of the rhythm of your breathing. If your breath seems shallow, begin to breathe a little bit deeper. Bring the breath all the way to your lungs. Don't be afraid to count to four as you inhale and count to four as you exhale. Start to connect to your five senses.

It's okay if your surroundings are loud and chaotic. You are going deep within yourself to find that peaceful place. I have heard of the mindful meditation practice being compared to the ocean.

Normally, we live on the surface of the ocean and we are tossed back and forth depending on the current state of the sea.

> **"** Grounding and meditating help to bring you into the deepest part of the ocean where it is calm. This is where we want to be.

We will never have control over our circumstances, but we do have the capability to go deep within and access the peace that transcends all understanding.

Intention: I will fight for you

This becomes a double mantra for me. As a mom, I am fighting for Jacob with every ounce of my being for his life, for his recovery. Fighting in prayer, fighting, fighting, fighting for him to stay alive. Then God is reminding me that he is fighting for me, too. He is fighting to give me peace, security, and reminding me that I am not alone.

I begin with bringing my intention to the forefront of my mind. Bringing the intention, *I Will Fight for You*, in my mind vehicle. As I look within, I begin to say this to myself.

I will fight for you is a promise I am hanging on to. I imagine God fighting for me to not completely lose it so that in turn, I can fight for my son. It takes everything in me to stay positive and hopeful.

I have to focus on trusting God as I begin to ruminate on this mantra. God is fighting for me. I inhale the intention, exhale any negative thoughts.

Visualization

I envision Jacob waking up. I envision him coming home, having a new lease on life. I envision him being an advocate for others who deal with depression and addiction. I envision him being an important voice for this generation.

Express Gratitude

I am so grateful for my friend, Lori. She had water and snacks delivered to our hotel room. I appreciate the thoughtfulness and her proactive approach to serving us in our time of need. It was a super sweet gesture that made a huge impact.

Beautiful Tragedy

Chapter 3 Surrender

"We must be willing to let go of the life we planned
so as to have the life that is waiting for us."

JOSEPH CAMPBELL

Being in the ICU, we are literally counting and measuring every breath Jacob takes, it makes me look at my health in a totally different way. It is humbling to see how we take our health for granted when we see the fragility of life. Grounding and being mindful today are very challenging, but I will continue to fight to stay present.

The doctors don't have good news.

They are telling us to prepare for the worst. We are still looking for the silver lining. I have to internalize the word, the mantra, the intention of surrender to permeate every cell, every fiber, in my body.

Day 3 is proving difficult to be still and stay in the moment. My anxiety is at an all-time high as the reality sets in that this is different from every other ER visit. I can't eat or sleep. I am finding it difficult to surrender. I fight to be in the moment. I need to meditate even more during this stressful time.

The doctor tells us that Jacob's EEG reports are not good. (EEG test records the brain wave patterns and the brain activity) He says that Jacob needs to do an apnea test to see if he can breathe on his own without the help of a respirator. Jacob needs to breathe on his own for five minutes, but he barely makes the two-minute mark, and they have to put him back on the respirator.

The doctor says we will try again tomorrow but if he fails it again, we will need to talk about arrangements for taking Jacob off life support. Wow!

Tomorrow is Father's Day. That is the day they are telling us that we have to pull the plug.

Erik is a wreck.

Years ago, a friend of mine had an experience where she flatlined during an ectopic pregnancy. The paramedics were at her house and she was pronounced dead on the scene. Robin recalled that she could hear the paramedics talking to her family. She could hear her husband crying in disbelief.

All the while, she could hear everything! She kept screaming in her head, "I am not dead, I am alive! Please God, let me stay, I don't want to go!"

When she reminded me of this story, we both agreed that she needed to share it with Jacob. Without hesitation, she sits beside him on the hospital bed, holds his hand, and begins to tell him her story. She keeps saying, "Just tell God you want to stay. Tell him you don't want to go yet."

Once she is done, she closes her eyes and sits in silence, still holding on to Jacob's hand. During these quiet seconds sitting quietly with him, she is suddenly overcome with sadness. It is a deep, gut-wrenching sadness that she feels is directly coming from Jacob. It is as if Jacob is responding, I don't want to stay, the pain is too much.

When Robin walks out of the room, she feels defeated. She is in disbelief as she relays Jacob's message to our family. Emma is the first person to hear this and is not surprised. She and Jacob have a very special bond and he confided to her many times that he was in too much emotional pain to go on. If anyone understands, it is our brave daughter, Emma.

This new information devastates us. We are ready to surrender.

We decide that we will take the time to be with Jacob one by one to say good-bye. We give him permission to leave, even though we don't want him to. We want him to know we love him deeply, but we understand if he doesn't want to stay.

Part what I have learned through the Grief Recovery Method® is to communicate all thoughts and feelings in order to bring completion. One of the explanations of grief is, "undelivered communication of an emotional matter."

One of the reasons we struggle with regret, guilt, and shame is because of the things left unsaid. We want to make sure each of us has the opportunity to share all that is in our heart. This is such a heavy night, but I have to surrender and trust the process.

G.I.V.E. Principle

Grounding

Breathe in and out. As you breathe, think of all five senses. Take a moment for each one and be grateful.

- I am grateful for my eyes, the ability to see the good in everything around me.
- I am grateful for my ears, the ability to hear and listen.
- I am grateful for my mouth, for the ability to speak, and taste.
- I am grateful for my sense of smell. The ability to smell the sweet aroma in the air.

- I am grateful for my health and the ability to breathe.

Intention: Surrender

With every inhale, I must bring the word *surrender* into my body. Beginning with my mind, I have to *surrender* all the mental anxiety I am feeling. All the runaway thoughts and all the worst-case scenarios. I have to *surrender* it all with every exhale.

It is a moment-by-moment choice to surrender.

Every time my heart rate speeds up, or my blood pressure rises, I choose to surrender and trust. I bring the word down to my heart.

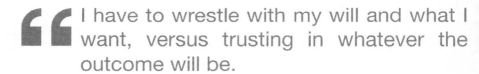 I have to wrestle with my will and what I want, versus trusting in whatever the outcome will be.

Surrender is the perfect intention for today.

Visualization

I work to visualize for the first time what my life would look like without Jacob. How will I live and go on with my life without him? It is painful and unbearable to even imagine, but I force myself to look at the inevitable outcome. I visualize myself having the strength and courage to live.

To be honest, I can't even imagine it.

Express Gratitude

It is especially important in this time of painful surrender, to focus on gratitude.

God, I am grateful that you loaned Jacob to me for the last 18 years. I am grateful I had the honor of being his mom. I am grateful that he was able to accomplish so much in such a short time. I am grateful to be here right now, holding his hand, kissing his face, and fully present while he is still alive.

Chapter 4 God Is With Us

"Never gotta stress cause' God's got my back.
I can't lose hope, I ain't goin' out sad."

HELLA SKETCHY "Stupid" (2018)

It is early in the morning of the fourth day. Our family is surrounding Jacob's hospital bed. We are fervently praying for a miracle. I am savoring every second with him, since today is going to be a very important day.

Today, Jacob needs to pass a breathing test called the apnea test. It would entail him breathing without the respirator for five minutes on his own. If he doesn't pass this test, we will have to talk about making arrangements to take him off life-support.

Today is Father's Day.

The feeling in the room is total despair and darkness. It is hard to grasp the reality of where we are. I keep wanting to wake up. The thought, 'this can't be real, this can't really be happening' runs on a loop through my head. Jacob is hooked up to tubes and machines and it is a hopeless scene.

The smell of hand sanitizer fills the air and the cacophony of machines beeping and ringing are on repeat. I fight to stay present as the reality of the inevitable feels like it is crashing in. I use my grounding techniques and begin to focus on my breathing. I can feel my heartbeat start to slow down. I sit next to my beautiful boy, and with one hand folded into his and the other caressing his soft youthful face, I am fully present.

I am alone in the room with Jacob when I receive a text from Gina. "I am in church right now and the pastor just said this, and it made me think of Jacob: 'God will fight for us even when we don't want Him to.' I know God is fighting for Jacob so hard."

I felt a new surge of hope fill my body. I stood up straight and puffed up my chest. This text gave me a ray of renewed hope.

Even if Jacob didn't want to fight, God is still in control and will fight for him. God is going to do the heavy lifting; Jacob just needs to surrender. I am reminded that God is more stubborn than Jacob. If God wants him to fight, God will not be stopped!

As family and friends begin to arrive, this becomes our theme prayer; our mantra for the day. God is with us!

Erik can overhear a conversation with the head doctor and the staff as they have an impromptu meeting outside our room. He hears them talking about Jacob, so he peeks his head around the corner a little bit further.

The doctor stopped in mid-sentence, looked my husband straight in the eye and asked, 'Are you Jacob's dad? Do you have any questions for me?' Erik is taken aback by this doctor's genuine concern and compassionate demeanor.

He tells the doctor that he is listening to learn more about the diagnosis. The doctor replied, 'I understand Jacob is supposed to have another apnea test today. Don't worry. We are not going to do that today. He's young; he's only 18; his organs are responding well. We're going to give him more time to heal.'

Erik begins to sob, and so do our family members who were within earshot of the conversation. I see everyone crying and I start to cry too, except I am not quite sure what everyone is crying about. I couldn't hear the doctor or anyone else for that matter; you see, I am really hard of hearing.

As everyone was hugging and crying, I finally asked, "Is this a good cry or a bad cry?" And through our tears we all burst out laughing, which was a welcome change to the somber feeling in the room.

Everyone is elated and celebrating that, at least for today, Father's Day, we are no longer thinking about taking Jacob off life-support!

Erik realizes that he never got the doctor's name, so he runs out to the hallway to find him, but the doctor was gone. He asked a nearby nurse, "Could you tell me the name of the doctor I just spoke with? I didn't catch his name."

"Oh, his name is Dr. Emanuel," she answered.

Once again, Erik bursts into the hospital room with his head in his hands, crying uncontrollably; so hard that he can't get his words out.

I think to myself, 'Oh no, what now!?' He proceeds to tell us the doctor's name….it is Dr. Emanuel. Wow!

The name, 'Emanuel', literally means God is with you! The energy in the room, especially around Jacob, suddenly changes and we are all filled with hope. God showed up and we feel him. God is with us!

G.I.V.E. Principle

Grounding

Be mindful of your posture during this session. Try to keep your back supported. Don't worry if your thoughts seem to be all over the place.

Start working through your breath. Inhale for a count of four and then exhale for a count of four. Start to observe your body language. Is your forehead furrowed? Is your jaw clenched? Are your shoulders tight and shrugged to your ears? With every exhale, melt a little bit more into your seat. Check in with your five senses. Be present.

Intention: God is with us

I inhale in the phrase: God is with us. With every inhale, I focus on bringing this intention directly in to my mind, body, and spirit. Beginning with my mind, I have to choose to intellectually believe that God is with me. There is no room for any other thought.

> If I go through the day looking at life through the lens of God being with me, then I will have confidence and security knowing that He will come through.

As I bring the words deeper into my heart and soul, I am reminded of all the other times God showed up for me. I have to believe that He can do it again. I continue to breathe in this phrase over and over.

Right now, I need this mantra to wash over me repeatedly, non-stop!

Visualization

With my visualization today I have renewed hope. Today, I really believe Jacob is going to wake up. I visualize his entire body being made new and whole. I imagine Jacob waking up with zero brain damage and being able to get back to his normal, goofy, loving self. Wake up, Jacob. We love you! The world needs you. Your work is not done here.

Express Gratitude

Wow! There is so much to be grateful for today. Thank you for bringing us an angel with Dr. Emanuel. Thank you for the hope that he brings to our family when we need it the most. Thank you that Jacob is responding and that he's continually getting better.

We are so grateful that we can be here, to be by his side and to love up on him. I think Dr. Emanuel is a little overwhelmed by all our hugs and excitement. We can't hold it in. He has given us the best Father's Day gift ever: HOPE.

Chapter 5 Renewal

"We have always held to the hope, the belief,
the conviction that there is a better life,
a better world, beyond the horizon."

FRANKLIN D. ROOSEVELT

Renewal is today's theme and it is much needed. After staying at the hospital all day and not eating or sleeping well, I need to be renewed and this meditation practice is renewing me day by day, if not moment by moment.

After an already eventful day, a friend of mine was getting ready to leave after being with us for the past 12 hours. Sandi is a powerful, spiritual prayer warrior and one of my best friends. She feels prompted to pray for Jacob and respectfully asks for our permission. What are we going to say, NO? There is no way we are going to do that! At this point, we are looking for as many prayers as we can get!

Sandi has us gather close together and we all crowd around Jacob's bed while she begins to pray. There are eight of us surrounding my beautiful son, each of us holding a part of his body. I am standing to the right of Sandi and I have hold of Jacob's right leg. Sandi is standing right by Jacob's head and she is holding his forearm.

As soon as the first words come out of her mouth, Jacob's body begins to convulse. His entire body starts to shake! As her prayers of deliverance intensifies, so does Jacob's shaking.

The ICU monitors start beeping out of control, Jacob's heart rate stats rapidly increase, and two nurses run to the door to see what is going on. There are also two other visitors that are behind the nurses and everyone just stands there, jaws dropped and completely still, like mannequins.

Sandi starts with her eyes closed, but when everything starts to intensify, she peeks at me with one eye open and I say, "Keep going!"

You can imagine the look on everyone's faces; we are all stunned into silence. This is like nothing we have ever seen or experienced before; it is like something from a movie! Sandi keeps calling various spirits out of Jacob's body: the spirit of despair, the spirit of depression, the spirit of addiction, and so on.

Jacob's body seems to have a visceral reaction to every word she speaks.

When Sandi is satisfied that all the spiritual afflictions are gone, she speaks to Jacob. "Ok. Now that the spirits are gone, we cannot leave you empty. You need to ask God to come inside of you. Ask Jesus to be your Lord and Savior and ask the Holy Spirit to come in."

At that very moment, the numbers on the monitors begin to stabilize. Jacob's body begins to relax, and when I open my eyes, I see tears flowing from his eyes.

Sandi congratulates Jacob by saying, "Great job Jacob, you did it! I am so proud of you!"

All I can say is, Wow! I have no idea what just happened, but it was pretty remarkable to witness. I am so glad there is a room full of people who also witnessed it, or I wouldn't have believed it myself.

The renewal of Jacob's faith is more important to me than anything.

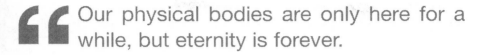 Our physical bodies are only here for a while, but eternity is forever.

I'll forever be indebted to Sandi's spiritual guidance and courage to obey the prompting of the Spirit to offer a life-changing prayer for our son.

From that point forward there is a definite change in the room's atmosphere, a lightness that had not yet been present. Everyone notices the difference, even though we can't describe it. Not only was Jacob's body being renewed, but more importantly, I can feel that his spirit was renewed and at peace with God.

No matter what your faith journey is or your spiritual belief, there are some things that just cannot be explained. As you can imagine, I was on such a high from that supernatural experience and I continued to share the story to anyone who would listen.

I am sure they thought I was crazy or delirious, or both!

The following morning was Monday and the head nurse came in to do her rounds and was busy writing on her clipboard, making no eye contact with me.

I begin to share the miraculous story of my friend praying over Jacob. I try to explain what happened with Sandi, the spirits, the shaking, and the monitors beeping out of control! Without turning her head to look at me, she said, "Oh, that's just seizures."

I say, "No, no, no. You don't understand. Something happened! Something no one can explain. There was a room full of people that witnessed it."

Then she looked up at me and said, "Nope. Just seizures." And walked out of the room.

Minutes later, the neurologist came in to give us the status of the EEG reports that were taken throughout the day on Sunday, including the time when Sandi was praying over Jacob.

So, I ask him, "From the reports taken yesterday, can you tell me if there was any seizure activity?" He looks intently at his charts, then looks up at me and says, "Nope, not a one!"

And that's when I knew with complete resolve, whatever happened in that hospital room was of God, and some things are not meant to be explained!

You see, we can choose how we want to view events in this world. We can tune out the idea of any spiritual input and try to scientifically rationalize absolutely everything...or we can ponder and embrace the exciting possibility that there is a much bigger picture to this life we live.

Albert Einstein said, "There are only two ways to live your life. One is as though nothing is a miracle. The other is as though everything is a miracle."

G.I.V.E. Principle

Grounding

Begin to breathe. Close your eyes. Inhale deeply, then exhale. With every breath, bring in new air, renewing the air in your lungs.

With every exhale, let all the worry and anxiety go. Start to slow down your heart rate with your breathing. Be mindful of your body language. With every exhale, melt a little deeper in your seat. Be aware of your hands; if palms are up, you are in the posture of receiving, if your palms are down, you are looking within for answers, discernment, and wisdom.

No judgment of yourself today. Just breathe.

Intention: Renewal!

It is Day 5! I am amazed at how resilient our bodies can be. I am learning so much about how our bodies are created to be renewed. Our bodies can heal, and it is miraculous.

Even though the mantra was intended for Jacob's renewal of his health and organs, I find myself seeking renewal of energy, faith, and strength daily. Inhale in renewal and exhale out all the negativity and fear.

Visualization

Today I am feeling complete resolve with whatever happens. Jacob's soul is going to be okay. I have full faith and I'm completely surrendered to God's plans. I visualize Jacob's body being renewed and increasingly regenerated with each passing day. I imagine him daily gaining more strength and becoming a miracle story that gives God glory and helps many people turn to Him.

Express Gratitude

I am grateful for the renewal of Jacob's soul and so grateful for my friends and family who witnessed this incredible day. I am grateful Jacob surrendered his spirit and let go of all the weight he was carrying. I am grateful that he is continuing to fight and that he is progressing. We are grateful for the baby steps!

Chapter 6 Regenerate

"Everything has seasons, and we have to be able to
recognize when something's time has passed and be
able to move into the next season. Everything that
is alive requires pruning as well, which is a
great metaphor for endings."

DR. HENRY CLOUD

Today I have one focus and that's to see Jacob's body
regenerate. We are hearing encouraging news from so many
people about friends, or family surviving near-death
experiences. Today, I am hopeful that Jacob will be one of those
miracle stories. The idea that our bodies, brain cells, and vital
organs can regenerate truly blows me away.

I am learning so much.

G.I.V.E. Principle

Grounding

Set your intention for your practice today. In times of
unbelievable trauma, you need to reset and regenerate your
thoughts. Our chatter can flood our bodies with so much
anxiety and worry.

I want you to start fresh. Sit here and breathe in through your
nose, exhale through your mouth. Be very deliberate and
intentional about inhaling and exhaling.

Once you feel like your breathing is calm, start to connect with your five senses. Go through each one, accompanied by your deep breathing. Take as much time as you need here.

Intention: Regenerate

We need Jacob's organs to regenerate, his kidneys are not bouncing back like they need to and while he is making progress, we are definitely not out of the woods.

Today I played this song over and over in Jacob's presence. It is a beautiful song from our worship team back home in Arizona. I'll leave some of the lyrics here.

REGENERATE! (A song from CCV)

Chorus

Hidden in you I find
There my soul awakening
In the spirit alive
What once was dead regenerate

Verse 2

When I wake
My eyes will see your face
I will rise and walk in faith
And I won't be afraid

Bridge

You awaken me
Bringing death back to life
In your shadows most high

Music is so beneficial in helping to regenerate our soul. I encourage you to play this powerful song. We played it on repeat and prayed for Jacob's organs to regenerate.

I am so thankful to our CCV family for this song that is healing and giving hope! This becomes our theme song.

Visualization

Today I envision every cell and fiber of Jacob's body regenerating, being made new, and bringing death back to life. I visualize 'liquid love' covering every part of Jacob's body, from top to bottom. I visualize miraculous healing and restoration.

Express Gratitude

Today I am grateful for all the love and support we are getting. It is quite overwhelming. I am grateful for our good friends who have come by to pray with us and pray over Jacob. They also brought us Panda Express. Yum! That is Jacob's favorite.

We are so overwhelmed that people have taken time out of their busy lives to be here with us. Thank you. It is truly humbling, and we are so grateful.

Chapter 7 Faithfulness

"Be faithful in small things because it is
in them that your strength lies."

MOTHER TERESA

Being in the ICU with Jacob and watching the medical staff carefully inspect every number connected to every organ in his body is chilling. It makes me aware of how I take my health for granted. The idea that our bodies are so unconditionally faithful to us, truly humbles me.

This is Erik's post on his social media today:

"Jacob is continuing to make progress. He is currently reliant on the respirator. His heart rate, temperature, and blood pressure are stable without meds. Please pray for the seizures to stop. He is currently on a dialysis treatment to help improve his kidneys and give him more time to recover. So that is our prayers and his fight right now. There are 3 scheduled dialysis treatments that will take place over the next 3 to 5 days. Your continued prayers and support are greatly appreciated. We love this boy so much!!!! Today is his sister's bday!!!! That would be the best bday gift. Please wake up, Jacob!"

After reading his post, I found myself struggling with my faith. *Was I in the same room as Erik? Why didn't I see all this progress he was posting about?*

I think as mothers, we have a sixth sense when it comes to our children. I can't tell you how many times I walked around that ICU praying for faith. I feel guilty for not sharing in my husband's optimism that Jacob is getting better. Rather, I actually feel like my son is doing worse, but I don't want to say it out loud. I want to have faith like my husband. I want so badly to believe.

My prayer is God, help me overcome my unbelief.

G.I.V.E. Principle

Grounding

In my grounding practice today, I focus on acknowledging the faithfulness of my sight, hearing, smell, and taste... and every organ.

Begin to connect your breath to your intention. Today our focus is on faithfulness. Think about the faithfulness of our senses as we connect our breath to our body. Take a few deep breaths here. When you think about how automatic it is for our hearts to beat or for our organs to work together, it is quite humbling.

Intention: Faithfulness

Being in the hospital I have become so acutely aware of how every organ, muscle, and bone work together so intricately. I am in awe of how everything works in sync with each other. Having Jacob on the respirator and literally counting each breath gives me a renewed gratitude for things I didn't even think about. Things I have taken for granted.

 I have to keep reminding myself to think good thoughts and choose to be faithful. Faith is action!

Today, I choose to stay on my path of visualization and mindfulness. Inhale faithfulness and exhale out any anxiety, doubt, and fear.

Visualization

I imagine Jacob miraculously waking up. I imagine him waking up and being ready to change his life. This would finally be his bottom. He will finally see the negative consequences of his drug use.

I visualize Jacob being a force in his sphere of influence and helping so many people who are struggling with addiction and mental illness. I visualize Jacob being passionate about his new purpose.

Express Gratitude

Even though it is harder today, I still find gratitude. Today, I am grateful that even through my fears and doubts, Jacob is still here. I can touch him, sing to him, pray with him, and dream with him. I am grateful for the staff and the doctors. I am grateful for the family and friends who have been faithfully by his side.

Chapter 8 Courage

"I learned that courage was not the absence of fear, but the triumph over it. The brave man is not he who does not feel afraid, but he who conquers that fear."

NELSON MANDELA

I woke up feeling panic and fear.

As soon as I get up, I can feel my heart beating out of my chest. It is as if every morning I hope to wake up from a bad dream, but then reality sets in and I am reminded that this is real life. I need courage today.

It is Day 8 at the hospital, and Sydney is so confused by the number of visitors flooding the ICU. She is wondering why grown men, rappers, producers, and family members buckle at the sight of Jacob and are crying so hard that they have to leave the room.

You see, in my daughter's 12-year-old mind, we've done this before. Jacob ends up at the hospital, stays a few days, then we go home. This time, she's putting it together that it might not be like all the other times. She pulls me aside and asks, "Mom, why is everybody crying when they visit?"

Then, with wide eyes, she innocently asks, "Does this mean Jacob might die?"

The air stilled for a moment as I try to know how to answer her. "What's the percentage?" she questioned.

I have to be as honest as possible: "Fifty percent."

I hold my breath waiting for her reaction. Just a small nod and then she shuffles in to sit by her big brother's side. With no warning, my heart is ripped from my chest as I hear my youngest scream in frustration and despair.

"Why? Why, Jacob? Please, no!"

I feel sucker-punched and helpless, listening to my daughter desperately beg her brother to live. It is beyond heart wrenching.

It is a horrible sound to hear your child cry out in despair, knowing there is nothing you can do to salve her indescribable pain. Jacob and his sisters have always been incredibly close, they love him so much.

We need a miracle…and soon!

G.I.V.E. Principle

Grounding

Begin by closing your eyes and imagining a white light shining on you. From the top of your head, imagine this light touching all five senses. We'll start with your eyes. Imagine the light that you see. The ability to see light and positivity wherever you go.

Next, your nose, imagine the light shining on your favorite scent, maybe a flower or candle. Then imagine the light illuminating on your favorite sounds, maybe the ocean, a waterfall, or a favorite song.

Now, imagine the light coming out of your mouth. The light that speaks life to those around you. Lastly, imagine the light all around you like a spotlight. Now just be still and breathe.

Intention: Courage

I have heard it said that courage is encouragement. When people encourage you, it is like they are putting courage in you. I am a life coach, wellness coach, leader, and I am usually the one pouring into others. Today, I need courage. I need encouragement. I am not ashamed to ask for it because I am on empty.

I post this on my social media today, asking for prayers:

"All my prayer warriors! Let's all collectively meditate on this passage!

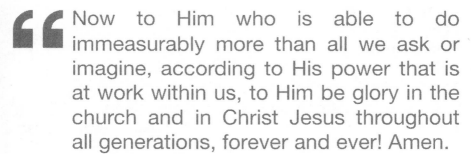 Now to Him who is able to do immeasurably more than all we ask or imagine, according to His power that is at work within us, to Him be glory in the church and in Christ Jesus throughout all generations, forever and ever! Amen.
EPHESIANS 3:20-21 NIV

The Bible says God can do more than we ask or can imagine, and we are asking for A LOT!!!! Please join me in imagining my sweet boy waking up and having no brain damage.

I pray and imagine that he defies every reason and statistic of his recovery. I pray that the only reasonable explanation is the miracle of God!!!

I am reminded of my daily mantra. Our intention is courage. What a joke. Courage is the last thing I am feeling. I feel weak, and I want to run and hide and never come back. I breathe deeply and realize that courage is not a feeling. It is an action. It is showing up even when I don't want to. It is being present in tremendous pain and facing it head on. That is courage.

I witnessed my beautiful, youngest daughter display that courage as she resolutely walked into Jacob's room to feel her grief at 100 percent. I am so proud of her.

Visualization

I imagine Jacob waking up. I miss his smile. I miss his wicked sense of humor. I envision him being okay, coming home, playing video games, being a kid. I imagine him once again playing pranks on his sisters. I imagine the three of them laughing together.

I love you. I need you to wake up. Please wake up.

Express Gratitude

Today I am grateful for Sydney. Her heart for Jacob is evident and it is too much to imagine how life will be without him. Despite the traumatic situation, Sydney continues to have a joyful, peaceful, optimistic heart. She is truly a beautiful soul and her presence makes us smile.

I am grateful for the beautiful relationship she has with Jacob. They have a special bond and they are hilarious together. I love how much Sydney trolls Jacob and gives him a taste of his own medicine! She inherited his wicked sense of humor.

I want to see their funny banter again. I want to hear him tell her poop jokes and watch his sister get so annoyed that she begins to chase him around, trying to punch him.

Chapter 9 Peace

"And the peace of God, which transcends all
understanding, will guard your hearts and
your minds in Christ Jesus."

PHILIPPIANS 4:7 NIV

I don't feel very peaceful today. I feel like we are running into
one issue after another. I am discouraged to see Jacob
weakening and today he looks really frail. He is being fed
through a tube and he is not able to process it.

We are looking for progress and today we are not getting any.
He had a dialysis treatment this morning and it is super rough
on his body.

Today I need extra supernatural peace. My anxiety level is at an
all-time high and I can feel my PTSD triggers and symptoms
start to flare. I feel like everything is caving in and suffocating
me. My heart keeps racing and I have this huge knot in my gut
that won't go away. I feel so overwhelmed. I am having a hard
time calming myself.

As I pray, my thoughts go to the last time our whole family was
together. We went to a gathering at Mosaic and heard a sermon
from Erwin McManus.

Jacob was so encouraged that his entire mood was completely
lifted, and we talked about him getting connected to that faith
community. Jacob always had a deep spiritual perspective, but
his new path really conflicted with the faith he was brought up

in. We tried to give him as much freedom to search and find his own way. I was super encouraged that he wanted to go to Mosaic with us.

I sent a message to pastor Erwin to say, "Thank You" and that I was so grateful that Jacob's last experience at his church was very positive and uplifting. I briefly explained that Jacob was in the ICU. I was extremely grateful that my son found a church community where he felt safe, not judged, and encouraged to pursue his creativity.

Erwin was out of the country at the time, but within just a couple of hours, Mosaic had campus pastors, Andres and Brooke, at the hospital to pray with our family and pray over Jacob. We were so blown away by their sacrifice to come visit us, even though we had never met.

They specifically prayed for God to give us the peace that transcends all understanding. I definitely feel like God answered my prayer. There is absolutely no reason at all why I should feel any peace today, but I do. It's only because of God's supernatural power! I am convinced of that.

G.I.V.E. Principle

Grounding

Begin by closing your eyes and taking a big inhale, then one full exhale. Start to focus on bringing your breath in deeper and deeper. Imagine your breath filling every part of your body from the top of your head to the bottom of your feet.

Keep your eyes closed and shift them to the right, to the left, up, and down. Be aware of the sounds you're hearing around you. Maybe it's quiet and tranquil, or loud and chaotic, start to identify the sounds you hear. No judgment, no expectation, just settle into your seat and relax. Connect to all five senses.

Intention: Peace

I am in desperate need of supernatural peace. I pray and pray until I can feel peace in my heart. With so many verses in the Bible reminding me not to worry, it doesn't take long until one comes to the forefront of my mind. I repeat it silently in my head until I feel the supernatural peace I crave.

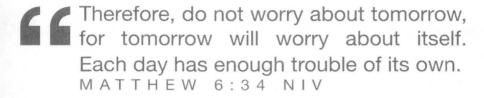

> Therefore, do not worry about tomorrow, for tomorrow will worry about itself. Each day has enough trouble of its own.
> MATTHEW 6:34 NIV

Visualization

I visualize myself feeling a deep sense of peace and security, no matter the outcome. I then visualize love being poured into Jacob by his family, friends, and supporters, and I envision him, too, feeling peace.

We are waiting for dialysis to help kickstart his kidneys to remove the fluid out of his body, so I envision Jacob being able to pee! C'mon bud, you can do this!

Express Gratitude

Today, I am grateful for the peace that transcends all understanding. I am grateful for Mosaic and the love they have shown us during this dark, tragic time. I am grateful for the campus pastors that dropped everything to come visit Jacob, even though we are not members of their community.

We feel so loved and cared for during such a tragic time.

Chapter 10 Love

"You care so much you feel as though you
will bleed to death with the pain of it."

J. K. ROWLING, *Harry Potter and the Order of the Phoenix (2009)*

It is early in the morning. The beeps and sounds of all the machines have become too familiar. It seems like they are competing to see who can be the loudest. The hospital smell of cleaning products fills the air.

Jacob is resting and he looks so peaceful. I feel his warm body and I give him kisses that would surely embarrass him if he were awake. He is extremely sedated and not responding. I just wish he could wake up and talk to me.

I slump down on the faux leather recliner seat in the room. It is not that comfortable, but it is better than the hard, plastic chairs strewn around the small space. I sit there going through old text messages between my son and me.

My heart smiles as I read our loving text exchanges. I am so grateful that I have taken every opportunity to tell him I love him, that I believe in him, and that I am always going to be there for him, no matter what. It is hard to imagine that we were just in L.A. ten days before we got the dreaded phone call.

We were there for a mini-vacation as a family. It was an amazing week. We were all so connected, so content, so close. We spent way too much money, but I didn't care because I knew that the memories we were making were invaluable.

At the time, I had no idea just how priceless they would be. Looking back, I feel God orchestrated the entire week, knowing this would be our last time together as a healthy, happy, whole family.

If Jacob was using at the time, it went completely unnoticed. I did look closely and wondered, but he never gave a hint of being under the influence. He promised us he was sober. We chose to believe him.

It was the last week of May and we had one of the best visits we have ever had as a family. We spent a lot of quality time together and Jacob was super engaged and wanted to spend time with us, which for a teenage boy, is a miracle of its own.

He initiated time with us, which was super special to me since he was extremely busy making music and filming videos for his album. He even wanted to go to church with us, which made me so happy.

When you bring a child up going to church, it is your greatest wish that they choose that path for themselves, that they find their own personal relationship with God. When Jacob shared with us that he found a place where he felt that connection, I was doing backflips on the inside, but of course, my outside stayed cool and collected. I didn't want to seem too excited.

My constant desire was for Jacob to feel whole and content, something that had been fleeting the last couple of years. A church that suited him would at least help him stay centered, I silently hoped.

When it was time to go, we hugged tightly, and he said, "I love you, Mom." It would be our last hug.

Reading his last text to me, he simply wrote, "I love you Mom. Just wanted you to know I was thinking about you."

G.I.V.E. Principle

Grounding

Begin your breathing practice. Regulate your breath and connect your breath to your five senses. Focus on love.

Being connected to your deepest self and taking this time to be present and intentional is a great form of self-love.

The moment you start to feel like this is boring, it's not helping, or it's a waste of time, is when you really need to carve out minutes to decompress and be still.

This is crucial, especially in traumatic situations that are beyond your control. At least you know that for the next few breaths, you can control inhaling and exhaling when nothing else in your world makes sense.

Intention: Love

I want to remember to tell my loved ones I love them every chance I get. We don't know what tomorrow will bring.

Don't wait until the conditions are perfect.

 Don't wait until you feel the other person deserves your love. Be the bigger person, say it first. I make it a point now to tell people I love them.

It's very uncomfortable. It's very vulnerable. But I have nothing to lose and I want people to know they are loved. Even though Jacob made choices I didn't agree with, one thing is certain, he knew I loved him unconditionally.

Visualization

I keep mentally replaying our last visit and I am so grateful it was all good memories. I keep visualizing the hug and the genuine, unprompted, "I love you."

I envision Jacob being full of love. Jacob loved people so deeply. I am so proud of the way he reached out to his friends and poured himself out. I visualize him with his friends again. Hanging out, playing video games, and making music.

I imagine him buckling over and laughing so hard his eyes disappear. I love you so much, Jacob. Mom loves you and I think about you all the time.

Express Gratitude

Today I am so grateful for Evelyn, Jacob's girlfriend. She is truly an angel. Evelyn has been by Jacob's side 24/7. Her strength and depth of character inspires me to no end. I am so grateful for their relationship.

She is everything I have ever prayed for in a girlfriend for Jacob. She is so kind, strong, compassionate, full of empathy, beautiful, authentic, bold, smart, and I could go on and on. Jacob was living with Evelyn for the last few months. It gives me comfort to know he was loved so deeply.

I am grateful to know that Jacob experienced true love.

Chapter 11 My Hope Is In You

"The theological virtue of hope is the patient and trustful willingness to live without closure, without resolution, and still be content and even happy because our Satisfaction is now at another level, and our Source is beyond ourselves."

RICHARD ROHR

Today my anxiety is through the roof. I know I need to calm my heart. I need to slow down and remember where my hope comes from. If I try to find hope in my circumstances, I will be on an emotional roller coaster, going up and down. If my hope is in God, I have security because God does not change.

We are in the waiting room with many visitors coming in and out. There are other families here visiting their loved ones. We were appalled to find out that while we had been at the hospital with Jacob, nine overdose patients had entered the ICU.

We watch them come in and out. One of the men two doors down is in his late forties and has overdosed many times before. We talk with his sister in the waiting room. You can see the despair in her eyes and the weariness in her face.

I remember thinking to myself, "Is this going to be our path if Jacob makes it through this ordeal? Oh God, please no."

I look at my daughter, Emma, as she listens intently to this woman. Later, Emma confided in me that she too had those same thoughts.

As we sit in the waiting room, we form a bond with the other families and share our snacks and drinks as we try to comfort them in our collective anxiety. We understand the feeling and we want others not to feel alone.

G.I.V.E. Principle

Grounding

Begin to deepen your breath. Be aware of the shallowness of your breath. Connect your breath to your senses. With every inhale focus on hope, with every exhale let go of any negative thoughts.

Go deeper into your soul and go through every fear you have…and let each one go.

Intention: My hope is in you

I am so grateful for the hope to go on, to believe in spite of the facts. I find hope and strength from God and His people.

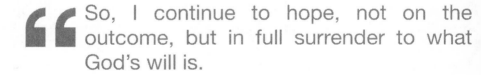 So, I continue to hope, not on the outcome, but in full surrender to what God's will is.

Any normal person looking at us would probably tell you that we are in total denial, and maybe even delusional. We do not accept what the doctors are saying.

We are not ready to let Jacob go. Not now, not anytime soon.

Our faith is bigger than the prognosis. I know for sure my mantra of the day helps to keep me afloat. I don't know where I would be without it.

Visualization

I visualize myself solid and strong. I visualize myself focused on God and His will. That no matter what happens, He is good, and He has a plan. I visualize myself in complete surrender to even the worst-case scenario: if Jacob doesn't make it, God will get me through it.

Express Gratitude

I am so grateful for my husband, Erik. As I watch him intently care for Jacob , have the hard conversations with the medical staff, and be so present, I am in awe.

I am blown away by how he continues to serve others, all our visitors, the medical staff, the waiters at the restaurant, the other people in the waiting room, while we are in ICU. I marvel at how he continues to pour himself out while living his worst nightmare. I am grateful to have a great role model of strength and service to others. I am grateful for how Erik loves his son.

I honestly don't know how Erik has the bandwidth to listen to the doctors and nurses, keep track of the procedures, medications, and everything else we have to do... I can't even tell you what time of the day it is. I've only seen Erik cry this hard once before, and it was when Jacob was born.

He was so overwhelmed with emotion holding his son for the very first time. Now he is wrestling with the reality of losing his one and only beautiful boy and possibly holding him for the very last time.

Beautiful Tragedy

Chapter 12 Rejoice

"Rejoice in the Lord always. I will say it again: Rejoice!"

PHILIPPIANS 4:4 NIV

After yesterday's barrage of bad news, we need hope today. The atmosphere in the room is somber. When the nurses come in, I can see the sad look in their eyes. Whenever I ask for updates, they say, "Miracles can still happen."

I want to believe so badly.

Today we need a miracle and God brought us Lyle and Langston Johnson. A friend of mine saw my post about Jacob's condition and contacted Lyle and her son, asking them to visit us in the hospital.

During his college years, Langston overdosed on heroin. He was taken to the hospital where he remained in a coma for 37 days! Lyle shared with us all the bad reports and how the doctors told them he wouldn't survive. If he did survive, he would live as a vegetable, never being able to do normal things, let alone play football.

They shared their story with us about how Langston defied every statistic and there was no real rational answer as to why he survived, let alone thrived. It was truly a miracle, one that we hoped for Jacob.

His story gave us an injection of hope we so desperately wanted. Langston gave us all the boost of faith that we needed.

I encourage you to watch his inspiring story. You can watch it here: **https://youtu.be/8uZpHzyBltc**. God knew that we needed hope, so he brought us this young man. I was in awe of their story and so grateful they took the time to share it with us.

Later that day, in my time with Jacob, I play a song from our worship team in Arizona, titled Rejoice. Part of the lyrics go, "Rejoice, rejoice oh my soul, He is good, He is always good to us." You can listen to the entire song here: **https://youtu.be/GMDGzE78u6w**.

This song is particularly meaningful because earlier in the year, Jacob and I went to the live worship concert together where they recorded this very song. It was during this particular song that I remember hearing the Holy Spirit say to me, "Until you learn that I am enough, you will continue to struggle. Even if the worst-case scenario happened, would I be enough?"

That question challenged me to evaluate my faith.

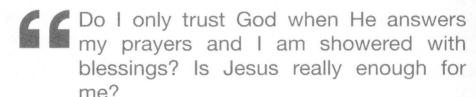

Do I only trust God when He answers my prayers and I am showered with blessings? Is Jesus really enough for me?

I wept and worshiped and committed myself to God once more and reaffirmed that He is more than enough. If I never get another blessing or if my prayers never get answered, He is still enough!

This is my Facebook post today:

"I am so heartbroken for my girls. They love their brother so much and it pains me to see them witness this. Their faith and strength carry me along with all your prayers. Today's mantra in my meditation practice is to lean into pain. Pain is a gift. It is a reminder of how big our hearts are and the capacity we have to love so deeply. My love for Jacob goes beyond limits of this physical world. There is no depth that I can even explain. I am grateful to be his mom and to have the honor and privilege of suffering such sorrow. Today I cry and it is okay. Pain is a gift. Lean into it. In a culture where we elevate happiness, I give myself permission to be sad today."

Pain and heartache are reminders of how much we truly love Jacob. I hope he can feel our love even though he is unresponsive. He is surrounded by so much love.

His girlfriend hasn't left his side. Every day more of his friends and family come to support him and wish him well. Jacob's friend, Bobby, even flew in from Austin, Texas to visit.

G.I.V.E. Principle

Grounding

Rejoice is a weird word to meditate on in the midst of such pain and trauma. Yet in the Bible, Paul calls us to rejoice always. In the book of Philippians, Paul is writing this book from prison, but his message is to rejoice!

As you begin your mindfulness practice, choose to rejoice. Shift your mind from worry and doubt to rejoicing. Rejoicing is a posture from within, not from our circumstances. Today I will be mindful of the details, the little things that make me happy. The fresh cup of coffee I get to drink in the morning, the way our family is handling tragedy with such grace and beauty.

Begin to inhale joy and gladness. Inhale all the beauty you see around you. I am grateful for every day we get to be with Jacob. Every day is a gift. Every day is a miracle. Exhale out all the stress and anxiety. Be present and go through all five senses with joy and gratitude for every single breath.

Intention: Rejoice!

We are going to rejoice and trust in God's plan. We rejoice in the beauty of life. Even in the wake of tragedy, we will rejoice!

Visualization

Today I am so inspired by Langston's story and recovery. If God did it for Langston, he could do it for Jacob. I envision Jacob waking up and being completely healed, without any trace of brain damage. I visualize every cell in his body repairing and regenerating. I visualize complete healing. I know God can perform miracles.

We saw one in Langston today, up close and personal. A real-life miracle. Amen!

Express Gratitude

Today we could not stop thanking Lyle and Langston for the much-needed hope they brought to our family.

I am grateful for the countless friends who come to visit, bring snacks, meals, and pray for us, and with us. I am grateful for Jacob's friends. I am grateful Jacob was surrounded by some pretty amazing people. I am grateful for my family and their constant support and strength. I am grateful for Jesus. He is truly my source of strength. I need him so badly.

Chapter 13 Lean Into Pain

"Behind every beautiful thing, there's some kind of pain."

BOB DYLAN

Being in the hospital I am looking at the bland, colorless, stale walls and feeling the chill of the cold air in the room. It is becoming more and more difficult to watch Jacob get poked, prodded, and hooked up to so many machines.

I want it all to go away. I am used to being able to just kiss the boo boo or put a band aid on his wounds and all would be well. But this moment just seems like it is never going to end, and the constant pain is too much to bear.

I want to simply wake up in another reality. I want to open my eyes and feel the flood of relief as I realize it was all just a bad dream. But it isn't and as much as I want to control everything and fix it, I cannot. Typically, if I cannot control something, I will try to numb the pain and not deal with it.

But that is not an option when my one and only son is hooked up to life support and I have no idea whether the next moment will be hope or heartache. I cannot run away from my son, even for a moment, because I might miss something. A twitch of a finger, a blink of an eye, any inkling that he is still there; that he is fighting to come back to us.

At times, the pain feels unbearable, like a weight on my chest cutting off my circulation. That is when I really need to lean into the pain, my current reality, and be fully present. I need to breathe deeply through the pain and the horrific realization that Jacob might not come back.

As I begin my mindfulness practice I engage with this present moment. I am fully aware of my temptation to check out, numb out, disassociate, and not be present because it is too painful. I will lean into the pain because pain is a reminder of how much I truly love Jacob.

G.I.V.E. Principle

Grounding

Today I choose to connect to what I am feeling wholeheartedly and connecting to the pain without trying to run away. Each day is beginning to feel like an eternity.

Breathe in new breath, new energy into the body, exhale out all the anxiety, worry, despair, depression, and whatever else is bogging you down. Without judgment and no expectations, tap into your safe place and settle into your seat. Feel your body start to relax with every exhale.

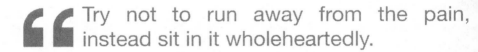 Try not to run away from the pain, instead sit in it wholeheartedly.

Some of us might feel very uncomfortable here because the feeling is very overwhelming. It's okay. Breathe through it and lean into the idea that life is tough right now. Begin to bring awareness and breath to all five senses. Lean into pain.

Intention: Lean into pain

As much as it hurts, as hard as it is, I will *lean into the pain*, I will not run away from it. To live wholeheartedly means we must be willing to feel the pain.

If I don't feel the pain, I won't have the ability to feel joy, either. It is a packaged deal. You cannot heal what you are not willing to feel.

Visualization

On this particularly long day I visualize Jacob being pain-free. I envision him without all the tubes and machines. I imagine him peaceful, healthy, and whole. I visualize our family united again, enjoying each other's company; going out to eat, laughing, listening to his new songs.

I want him to wake up so badly.

Expressing Gratitude

Today I am grateful for the medical staff. The care that Jacob is getting is exceptional. I feel like they truly care. Some of the nurses are so invested in Jacob that they come by to visit and check in on him even when it's not their shift.

I am grateful for their compassion, crying with us, being in the trenches with us during this nightmare. I am grateful we are living in a time where modern medicine is helping my son stay alive so we can be with him for another day. I am grateful that we can cherish every second with Jacob.

Chapter 14 | Need To Borrow Your Faith

"We're all just walking each other home."

RAM DASS

Today I feel empty. I feel like a shell. I feel like I am in the *Twilight Zone*. The hospital walls are making me feel claustrophobic and the mood hanging in the air is a feeling of hopelessness.

Some of our longtime friends come to visit and they make us get out of the hospital for a change of scenery. We walk over a couple blocks to a restaurant and try to escape reality for a bit.

It is a nice break from the monotony of being in the hospital. It seems like all we do is wait for good news and we wait for it minute by minute.

Prayer is the most important thing we can do right now. We ask people from all over the world to pray for Jacob to wake up. Gina shares a beautiful visual with us during dinner. She says,

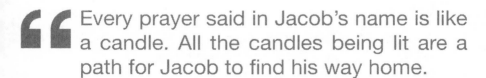

> Every prayer said in Jacob's name is like a candle. All the candles being lit are a path for Jacob to find his way home.

I envision Jacob coming home soon. If not my home, then God's home.

G.I.V.E. Principle

Grounding

Begin by bringing awareness to your breath. Inhale deeply and create space in your chest, lungs, and belly. Slowly, exhale out everything that you don't need. Do this a few times and start to listen to the rhythm of your breath.

Notice areas in the body that feel tense or tight. Bring oxygen to those areas of the body and start to relax. As you connect the breath to all five senses, make a decision to be present and in the moment. Even if it's just for the next fifteen minutes.

Intention: I need to borrow your faith

In my mindfulness practice today, I really have to force myself to be still and breathe. It feels irresponsible to sit still for fifteen minutes when everything else feels out of control. But that's just it, there is nothing anybody can do at this point because the only one who is truly in control is God.

It doesn't matter that we have the best doctors, facilities, treatment, machines, all of it; there is nothing we can do at this very moment except wait. Wait on God.

All I can do right now is breathe. Inhale through my nose and exhale out through my mouth. Even breathing feels like such a hard task right now.

In the midst of my anxiety I focus on regulating my breath and not freaking out. I am tapping into my inner strength, my peace, my safe place. I am connecting my breath to all five senses, letting go of fear and anxiety with every exhale. I imagine it exiting my body every time I breathe out.

Once I get my breathing somewhat regulated, I begin to set my intention for my meditation practice. *"I need to borrow your faith."*

I say that phrase over and over. I am not sure who exactly I am borrowing this faith from, but I am willing to borrow from anyone who has some to spare.

As I sit here, I let out a huge sigh. I feel like I am running on empty and don't think I can take another moment of this. I have nothing left.

Every morning I pray for strength and surrender. I get my heart to a place of trust and say, "Okay God, so be it, whatever You decide with Jacob, I will surrender. He is Yours and he was only on loan to me anyway. Thank you. I will be at peace with whatever You choose."

That feels easy when I am in prayer one-on-one with God, but as soon as I step into the hospital room and see Jacob breathing and his heart beating, I can't do it. I take everything back. "I can't do it. I can't let him go. I take it back. I am not ready. I am begging You to let him wake up. God, please don't take him!"

I am surrounded by strong, faithful friends and family and they carry me by loaning me their faith today. They are carrying me right now. Borrowing requires asking, asking requires humility. I have never been so humbled.

All I can do is ask.

I am asking fervently for prayers and I literally feel the strength of every prayer being lifted up. Once again, I start to feel the peace that transcends all understanding. That peace is not something that stays once I find it. It is a continual process to stay in that mindset.

Sometimes I can get there through my own prayers, but sometimes, like today, I need the help of others. Today I ask because I am empty.

Visualization

I visualize many prayers being offered up to God not only for Jacob, but for our family. I cannot tell you exactly what it looks like, but I can tell you that I feel the strength from every prayer offered.

Today I do not think I am going to make it. It is hard to breathe. I am in the middle of breaking down. I am convinced that the only reason I don't is because of people's prayers. Thousands of people are praying.

Our posts are being shared throughout social media. Jacob's fans are praying. It is a beautiful thing to behold.

Express Gratitude

I am so grateful for my relationship with God. God has walked with me through this difficult tragedy and has often carried me when I felt like I couldn't take another step. I am grateful for God's words which feels like a balm to my soul. When no other words can comfort me, the Bible seems to penetrate my innermost parts. I am grateful for the Holy Spirit that comforts me when nobody else can.

The Bible says the Holy Spirit intercedes for us in prayer when we have no more words. I am grateful for Jesus because he gave up his life for us, even when it was hard, and when everything was against him; he surrendered. In darkness I find intimacy with God like never before. I need you, God!

> " Even though I walk through the darkest valley, I will fear no evil, for You are with me; Your rod and Your staff, they comfort me.
> PSALM 23:4 NIV

Chapter 15 Forgiveness

"It's one of the greatest gifts you can give yourself,
to forgive. Forgive everybody."

MAYA ANGELOU

Everyone is distraught and feeling helpless. You can feel the tension in the air. We have been at the hospital all day and everyone is restless.

Evelyn is struggling because she keeps replaying that terrifying morning in her head over and over. She is having a hard time forgiving herself. I reassure her that it's not her fault. Her quick reaction actually gives us a miracle of being able to have extra time with our son.

We are grateful for every second we have with him.

Jacob's tattoo artist and his girlfriend came to visit today. Jacob was actually supposed to get a tattoo the night he overdosed, but Jesse had to reschedule because he had plans.

He keeps wondering if things would be different right now if he didn't cancel his plans with Jacob. He feels responsible that he wasn't there that night, that maybe he could have prevented it.

I look Jesse straight in the eye and say, "As Jacob's mother, I want you to know that you were exactly where you were supposed to be that night and Jacob was exactly where he was supposed to be. It is not your fault. I need you to let that go."

With tears in his eyes, he nodded, but I could feel his despair. So many other friends came by to express similar thoughts, like "If only... what if?... we should have..."

All of these things are not helpful now. I forgive all of them, I forgive everyone. There is not one person responsible. At the end of the day, Jacob chose to take those drugs. That is the harsh reality. I forgive him, too.

G.I.V.E. Principle

Grounding

Forgiveness and grief go hand in hand. A lot of times, unforgiveness will keep us stuck in our grief. You see, grief is energy; forgiveness is energy. Once you release that energy, you can move forward.

Today I focus on forgiveness. With every breath and every inhale, I focus on forgiving. With every exhale I focus on letting it go. I know it is not easy.

Intention: Forgiveness

I forgive Jacob today for taking the drugs and putting himself in this situation of fighting for his life. I forgive the people around him that contributed to his using. I forgive the person or people who actually gave him the drugs. I forgive all the professionals who couldn't help our son. I forgive some of the staff at the hospital whose bedside manner lacked the compassion and empathy that I felt Jacob deserved.

Most importantly, I forgive myself for not knowing how to help my son. I forgive myself for not saving him.

Inhale forgiveness and release all these people with love.

As I breathe, I connect to all five senses, focusing on forgiveness.

Visualization

One of the most important things I learned in Grief Recovery is that you cannot be complete without the truth. I have to be completely honest with myself and others in order to move forward. I can truly say with 100% certainty that I find forgiveness in my heart for all the people involved.

All the enablers, dealers, friends who used drugs with Jacob, and friends who should have said something. Most importantly and probably the hardest is to find forgiveness for myself. For not protecting Jacob, for not saving him. I visualize setting all of these people free, including myself.

One by one, I go through each person, visualizing their face, and letting them go.

God gives me an important vision. One that finally releases me from the judgment and shame I felt about myself. I realize that there are people out there who will judge my parenting choices and judge what I should have or shouldn't have done for Jacob. Sadly, many of these judgments will come from people who have no idea what was happening behind closed doors.

At this point, there are already many hurtful comments and posts made online about our family. Unfortunately, I am not surprised that many of the judgments will come from people close to us, even from our own faith community. It is okay.

I have made peace with knowing people will judge. There is nothing anyone can say to me that is going to hurt me more than what I am feeling right now.

A question was asked to me. "If you knew then what you know

now, would you have let Jacob go to Los Angeles to pursue his music career?"

I pondered that question heavily. The answer is YES. I may be accused of a lot of things, but there is one thing I am sure of, I love Jacob Tyler Thureson with my whole heart. So much so that I was willing to give him the freedom to live his life and make his own choices. When I look at how much God loves me, I am reminded that He gives me freedom every day. He doesn't try to control or force me to follow Him.

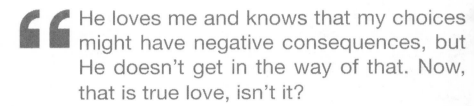 He loves me and knows that my choices might have negative consequences, but He doesn't get in the way of that. Now, that is true love, isn't it?

So, when I look at the freedom God gives me, it is not because He doesn't care, it is because He truly loves me. My heart is broken into a million pieces right now. I hope Jacob knows without a shadow of a doubt that I love him so deeply.

I just want him to hear me say it one more time.

Express Gratitude

I am grateful for today. I am grateful for the freedom that forgiveness brings. I am grateful to be able to release all bitterness and unforgiveness in my heart.

Keeping those feelings in my heart will only lead to resentment and regret. I am grateful to all the teachers, preachers, and leaders that have given me inspiration and guidance.

I am grateful for the tools I've learned over the years that help me to keep my heart, mind, and spirit clear.

Chapter 16 It's Not Over

"Stop acting as if life is a rehearsal. Live this day as if it were your last. The past is over and gone. The future is not guaranteed."

DR. WAYNE DYER

Today is one of those mornings.

I arrive at the hospital to find Jacob in a fairly stable state. I am happy and relieved after the rough night he had before. His breathing is stable and there is a calmness in the room. We sit as a family, having coffee and chatting quietly.

Everything almost has a sense of normalcy, as if we are sitting around the living room on a Saturday morning just enjoying each other's company.

It is a welcome change after a hectic and stressful last few days.

A short time later, the neurologist comes in to deliver an update. He pulls us into the waiting room and my heart leaps to my throat in fearful anticipation. He comes to deliver very bad news. He says we need to make arrangements for the inevitable and at this point, it is only a matter of time. He reiterates that the EEG reports are showing rapid brain deterioration and that his body is no longer responding.

All of the hope we had left is gone, and the doctor is very combative and seems angry as he delivers the news.

I don't know if he was annoyed at our sunny optimism and he wanted to tell it to us straight, or if he was just tired of the senseless overdoses he continued to see in the ICU. He kept reminding us that it was only a matter of time until the inevitable was going to happen.

I watch Erik handle him with so much grace and kindness, asking him questions and being so calm even though the doctor is obviously feeling agitated. I, on the other hand, refuse to listen to the man and tune him out altogether.

It is hard to reconcile the words he is saying. I am beside my sweet boy, watching him as he sleeps, looking like an angel with his beautiful bright pink hair. I can see him breathing, I can feel his warm skin. What is the doctor talking about?

My sister, Marty, is leaving tonight, heading back to Seattle. She has been an amazing support by our side the entire time. After this update, she walked into Jacob's room with Emma.

They stood on opposite sides of the bed, each one holding one of his hands as they spoke to him. Marty watched Emma talk to her brother and although Jacob's eyes were open just a sliver, she could clearly see that he was looking straight at his sister when she was speaking to him.

Marty was on the opposite side of the bed and told us that she asked Jacob to look at her. He turned slightly in her direction and looked at her face!

Once more she asked him to look at her…and he did it again!

Crying and shaking, she ran out of the hospital room to find us in the waiting room. Without warning, I hear my sister yelling very loudly, "F*#! the neurologist! He looked at me! I asked him to look at me and he did it!"

By now she has the attention of everyone in the waiting room.

My jaw drops. Partly because Jacob looked at her, but mostly because my sister cussed. If you know Marty, she doesn't cuss. Ever! But she was absolutely elated by what she had experienced!

Jacob had given her a a priceless gift.

I run into the room to see for myself. I beg Jacob to look at me. I ask him to squeeze my hand. I am searching for a message. But there is nothing. While I am happy for Marty's experience, I am disappointed that I didn't see it for myself. She left that evening with so much hope that I will borrow some of it.

We ended that day on a positive high. It's not over and we refuse to give up!

G.I.V.E. Principle

Grounding

Today is an important day. I must clear my head so I can go to the hospital prepared to fight the battle another day. I am not only seeing the value and importance of the **G.I.V.E. Principle**, but I feel the difference when I don't meditate.

The stressful times when I think I don't have time are totally when I need it the most.

Sit and connect to the breath. Bring awareness to your senses. Let it all go and focus on the rhythm of your breath. Breath is my ammunition to go into battle.

The root word of Spirit in Hebrew is *rucha* or *ruach* which means "breath." What a cool visual.

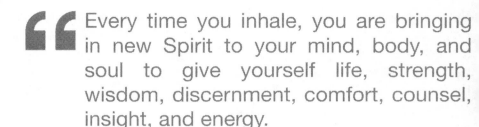

Every time you inhale, you are bringing in new Spirit to your mind, body, and soul to give yourself life, strength, wisdom, discernment, comfort, counsel, insight, and energy.

Intention: It's not over

This morning I wake up groggy and I need to clear my head before I return to the hospital prepared to fight the battle. I don't want to meditate, I just want to get to Jacob's side, but I know the value and importance of making these 15 minutes a priority.

I feel the difference when I don't meditate, my family feels the difference. My decisions are different, my reactions are different. The sense of being overwhelmed will only compound if I don't take those 15 minutes.

The stressful times when I think I don't have time (or don't want to make the time) is absolutely when I need it most. Today is definitely one of those days. I internalize this mantra over and over. It's not over. Please, it cannot be over. I beg you.

Visualization

During my visualization, I remind God of something. "Okay God, you raised Jesus from the dead in three days, Lamar Odom came back from a near death coma in eleven days, Langston Jackson came back after 37 days. We believe you can do anything!!!"

I visualize the faces on the medical staff when Jacob miraculously wakes up! I imagine the looks of disbelief on the faces of the doctors and nurses. I especially love visualizing the neurologist's expression. Oh, what a glorious day that will be!

I imagine sharing God's miracle with everyone. One of Jacob's doctors said in his 20 years of working in the ICU he has only experienced seeing two people near death wake up with no medical explanation. I imagine Jacob being his third. We are still hoping for that. We are still expecting miracles! It's not over!

Express Gratitude

I am grateful that today is a good day for Jacob. The last couple of days have been so rough with dialysis treatments and nonstop seizures. I am grateful for a day of relative calmness.

I am grateful that Marty and Emma got to see Jacob looking at them; and that my sister flew back home to Seattle with that assurance of love.

I am grateful for the constant strength of everyone around me and that we have one more day with Jacob. Every day is a miracle and every day is a gift.

Today I am grateful for my family. They are so strong and have been by my side. My family and friends come to support me, and I am so grateful for their presence. My beautiful niece, Tani has faithfully been by Jacob's side.

Chapter 17 Hope

"There is a saying in Tibetan, 'Tragedy should be utilized as a source of strength.' No matter what sort of difficulties, how painful experience is, if we lose our hope, that's our real disaster."

DALAI LAMA XIV

My cousin came to visit and so did some of Jacob's friends. We decide to go out for a quick dinner. None of us want to leave Jacob's side, but our friends insist. "You guys need to get out and get fresh air, it will be good for you."

Normally we would have someone stay behind in shifts. Tonight, everyone agrees that we all need to recharge and get outside into the real world. We all say good-bye to Jacob. "We'll be right back, we're only going out for a bit, we love you."

Erik forgot his water bottle, so he went back into the room. As he was leaving, he leaned into Jacob and said, "Just so I say it, you are totally and completely forgiven, there's no shame or judgment, only love. We just want you to get better. We love you. See you soon, we'll be right back."

We go out for sushi. It is nice to get out of the hospital and have a change of scenery. While in the middle of dinner, I get a missed call from the hospital. I excuse myself and call them back.

It's the nurse.

"Jacob's heart stopped. We were able to do CPR to revive him, but you guys should come back ASAP."

I panic and tell everyone we need to go back. Erik looks at me with tears in his eyes, and he's wondering if forgiving Jacob was the last thing Jacob needed to hear before he could depart.

We scramble out of the restaurant, leaving half-eaten meals on the table. By the time we get back, Jacob is stable, but his breathing is labored. He is struggling. His blood pressure drops dramatically, and they give him medicine to help stabilize him.

At this point I am feeling anxious about my son's condition. He looks so different tonight than how he looked this morning. It is so hard to see my child in pain. I wish I could take it away. I wish I could trade places with him. We continue to wait in hope and expect a miracle. It's not over 'til it's over and we are not giving up hope.

G.I.V.E. Principle

Grounding

Hope. Hope is powerful. Hope gives us something to hold on to. The Webster's definition of hope is this: "A feeling of expectation and a desire for something to happen."

As I breathe today, I think about hope. What do you hope for? I breathe in hope for Jacob to wake up and exhale out any doubts or negative thinking. There is no room for doubt. Jacob needs every ounce of our faith! I will choose to have hope today, no matter what. I will connect my breath to all five senses and every single time, my focus is on hope.

Intention: Hope

Hope comes after suffering.

> **" "** Not only so, but we also glory in our
> sufferings, because we know that
> suffering produces perseverance;
> perseverance, character; and character,
> hope.
> ROMANS 5:3-4 NIV

I meditate on this passage of Scripture today. I realize that in order to get to the hope, I must first go through suffering. Once I surrender to the suffering, I must persevere…and that means I can't give up.

I am trying my hardest to not give up.

Isn't it interesting that we all want hope, but don't want to suffer? I know I don't!

This whole process is so painful, but in a weird, inexplicable way it feels like every day that we persevere and not give in to doubt, we get stronger. It's like getting a really good workout at the gym; it's so hard, you're so sore, but in the end you get stronger.

That's how I have felt. So weak and frail during this journey but now I am starting to feel hopeful and strong.

Every moment is a temptation to just say, "Let Jacob rest, he's gone through enough."

But my faith will not allow defeat. We are going to fight with everything we have, and God will get the final say. As long as there is still breath in his lungs, there is still hope.

Today I choose to have hope.

Visualization

I visualize my beautiful boy feeling peaceful and calm. I imagine him feeling complete comfort. I hope he is not feeling too much discomfort. I want him to feel all of our love and support. I imagine covering him with my love like a warm blanket.

I envision Jacob as an eight-year-old precarious, energetic child. He has such charisma and charm. He is so likable. I don't think he has ever had an enemy.

Why is this happening to such a sweet kid?

What could it be that hurt him so much that he felt drugs were the only escape?

I will never know the answers to these questions. I can choose to remember Jacob in his purest, happiest, form, and hope that inside his shell of a body, he is feeling vibrant and full of life in his spirit.

Free from pain, depression, anxiety, and addiction.

Express Gratitude

Gratitude shifts our perspective. The more we focus on the dreadful news, the bad reports, and the statistics, the more bad news we get. If we focus on the positive, we can open our eyes and minds to the endless possibilities of things we haven't even thought about yet.

Our focus is on Jacob's recovery and comfort. It is especially important after nights like tonight to understand and practice gratitude. I am grateful Jacob is still fighting.

I am so proud of him. He's so strong and such a fighter.

I am grateful for all the love and support from friends and family. I am grateful for the way his music community has come together to pray and support Jacob's complete healing and restoration.

Beautiful Tragedy

Chapter 18 It Is Finished

"The pain of parting is nothing to the joy of meeting again."

CHARLES DICKENS

We spent all night at Jacob's bedside. It was touch and go.

I need to breathe, but the air in the room feels so thick around me that I can barely suck it in. I feel the pressure of oxygen squeezing in around me.

How can I stay mindful and present during such a traumatic event? My insides are screaming. My chest is burning. I want to control the situation. I want to turn back the clock. I want to start over, knowing all I know now! But these wishes are all in vain.

I can do nothing but breathe. Breathe and try to stay present.

As we sit staring at the monitor, watching his heart rate, watching his blood pressure rise and fall, it is as if we are watching a suspenseful movie on Netflix with every passing minute being a cliffhanger. Except it is not a movie. I wish it was.

I am struck by a memory. I think back to my first ultrasound appointment, when I saw my firstborn's heartbeat on the monitor. How miraculous. Jacob was just a little bean at the time. No name, no gender. Just a perfect little heartbeat that meant he was real.

I remember staring at that little bean and feeling awestruck and wondering what would lie ahead for this little human.

For a second, I wish that I could go back there, but I know it wouldn't be the same and I wouldn't want to erase a second of this life my son has led. Jacob has been nothing short of brilliant. I would have loved to take away his pain, but to do so would have taken other parts of him and who am I to change God's masterpiece?

Jacob was created with intention and perfection. Perhaps his time was limited but that doesn't negate the purpose of his spirit, the journey of his life.

Just as the monitor showed me the start of his life, it now shows me the end. As we watch the heart monitor and observe Jacob's blood pressure go down, we sit in this surreal bubble on pins and needles holding our breath.

At about 1:00AM, Jacob's blood pressure drops dangerously low. He is given a shot of dopamine to bring him back.

Our entire family is in the room, feeling helpless, watching, and waiting. Once again, they administer medication and get him stable. I thank God for more time with my precious boy. Every second is a gift, and we are grateful for every single one that passes, even though we wish time would stop right now. We all sit in silence, exhausted and scared.

Most of us are barely awake. Some of us are sitting in chairs, a few of us are sprawled across the cold hospital tile floors and Erik is pacing just outside the room.

The time is now 5:00AM and the monitors begin beeping again.

I can hear the panic in the nurse's voice, "He's coding, I need help in here!"

Now she is screaming out other technical terms. I don't understand any of the words, but every fiber of my being feels her panic and fear. It is complete pandemonium in the room.

My niece takes Sydney out of the room. We nervously ask her to get Erik from the waiting room. Erik must be here. It is time for him to come back into the room. I watch in horror as they conduct CPR again. With all their might, they pounce on Jacob's chest, thrusting with incredible force.

Where's Erik!?

The violence of it causes my legs to give out and I drop to the floor in hysterics. Without thinking, words rush from my mouth. "Why are you hurting him? Why are you hurting my son?"

The moment we dreaded and feared the most has arrived.

I don't think I can live through it.

Where's Erik!?

I want the universe to suck me away to nothingness. It is beyond anything I can possibly bear.

There are sounds coming out of my mouth that I never experienced before. It is as if the moans and groans are coming directly from the deepest parts of my soul, in utter agony. I am hysterical.

I cannot bear to watch them conduct CPR. The process is too intense and agonizing. I am inconsolable.

Erik has entered the room, but I can't get to him.

Family members and medical staff are trying to hold me and the only person I allow to console me is Emma, my 17-year-old daughter. She is so unbelievably strong. Emma is shaking uncontrollably and crying as she holds me.

"It's going to be okay, Mom, it's going to be okay." I look in her eyes and see her mature light years right before me.

'This isn't fair'. Emma shouldn't have to be this strong for everyone. In her relationship with Jacob, she always had to be the strong one. At one point, one of the nurses walks over to make sure she is okay.

This kind and compassionate nurse is consoling us and reminding us to breathe. They are able to revive Jacob again and the head nurse asks us if we want to resuscitate him again, should the need arise.

Erik looks at me with a painful expression of resignation, and all I could say was, "Please stop hurting my baby. Why are they hurting him? Make them stop!"

At this point, we all know what is going to happen. One by one, the medical staff slowly walks out of the room. They are walking in slow motion, like what you would see in the movies, except it wasn't.

The room melts back to being just our family. We approach Jacob and surround him with all the love we have in our hearts. The violent storm of emotion calms, the waves settle, and a warm blanket of peace floats down on all of us.

We look at Jacob with every memory flooding our hearts and minds, almost as if time stood still for us. Every precious moment of Jacob's life settled there in our circle. All the joy, all the tender pain, all the music he created, all the caring he poured out to others.

At this point, Emma is still shaking violently, she can't stop. As soon as she reached her hand and touched Jacob's hand, her body miraculously stilled, and peace came over her.

The rest of us followed. Erik, Evelyn, Karen, and I make our way to Jacob. We surround him and Erik reaches in to rest his right hand on Jacob's heart. As he prays for our family and for himself, he feels his son's very last heartbeat.

And with that final heartbeat we surrender to the finality of Jacob's life. We weep. It is a beautiful moment.

As tragic as it is, it is our family's beautiful tragedy.

G.I.V.E. Principle

Grounding

The fight to stay present has never been as difficult as today. The idea that today could be Jacob's last makes me want to run far away and not be here. I breathe. I stay. I brace myself for what is to come. I remind myself to connect to myself.

Intention: It is finished

Although today is the hardest day of my life, I feel a calm surrender knowing that it is over. It is finished. Jacob came to this life with a purpose. I may not agree with the duration of his life, but I trust that he finished his purpose here. This is a painful reality for me.

Visualization

It is finished. Jacob is free. He is now free from pain and suffering. He is free from the struggle of depression and addiction. The visualizations I have been having this entire time are now coming true, just not here on this side of heaven. I imagine, and know wholeheartedly, that Jacob is complete once again.

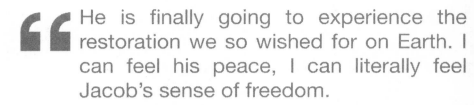 He is finally going to experience the restoration we so wished for on Earth. I can feel his peace, I can literally feel Jacob's sense of freedom.

And with tears streaming down my face, I imagine Jacob finally going home.

Express Gratitude

As horrific and tragic as tonight has been, I am filled with an amazing sense of silent, unspoken gratitude. I am grateful to be Jacob's mom. I am grateful he was entrusted to Erik and me, albeit for too short a time.

I am so grateful we are all able to experience this together. The way that God brought so many people together to pray and support Jacob is astounding!

I am in awe of the incredible love that has been shown to our family. And surprisingly, I am even grateful for the pain…it is an indicator of how deeply we loved Jacob.

Chapter 19 Numb

"There is a level of grief so deep that it stops resembling grief at all. The pain becomes so severe that the body can no longer feel it. The grief cauterizes itself, scars over, prevents inflated feeling. Such numbness is a kind of mercy."

ELIZABETH GILBERT

Today is the first day without my first-born son.

The first day of a world I don't want to belong to. Just being able to breathe today is an accomplishment. That is all I can muster up today.

We are staying at our friends' house in Los Angeles while they are away on vacation. I do not want to be here. I want to be back at the hospital with my son. I want to be back in that room, holding his hand and stroking his hair. But that time has passed, and a new, strange world lay before me. Our generous friends have taken such great care of us.

When we wake up early in the morning, Erik is distraught and can't sit still. I am numb, lying in bed, paralyzed with fear. Erik wants to leave; he can't stay in the house any longer.

Our friends have two younger children and the sounds of laughter and little feet running around the house is too much for him to bear. He is having flashbacks of what life was like when Jacob and Emma were little, and their laughter filled the house.

I can't move, so I just lay in the dark room, motionless, and utterly numb.

I am numb. I am in shock. I am in disbelief. I am trying to figure out what to do next. I breathe in, exhale, pray and somehow gain the supernatural strength to communicate the news to everyone. I post this on my social media:

"You are not supposed to go before your father or grandfather. That's not supposed to happen. That's not how this works. We have no words.

"We are so sad to share that Jacob Tyler Thureson passed away on June 27, 2019 at 5:11 a.m.

"Jacob was found unresponsive on June 13th from an apparent drug overdose. He was revived and brought to the ER where he's been in a coma for 14 days.

"Never in a million years would I have imagined that it would end like this. The opioid epidemic does not discriminate. The conversation regarding drugs, depression, mental illness, social media, needs to be happening more openly without judgment and stigma.

"We will not waste this pain; our pain is our platform to magnify this important conversation. Jacob's life was not and will not be in vain. The last two weeks have been a gift. Jacob flatlined for what could have been up to 35 minutes, and to be believe that we were able to share these last two weeks with him has been a miracle.

"Every day many miracles happened! So many lives touched. Jacob had so many people turning to God in prayer. There was incredible unity from people of all backgrounds with one hope and that was for Jacob to pull through.

"We might not understand why we go through these dark moments, but we do know that no matter what, God is still good, and we praise Him.

"We love you, Jacob. More than words can express. We honor your short 18 years of life, and we promise, your legacy will live on forever."

G.I.V.E. Principle

Grounding

Inhale, exhale. Seems like such a monumental task. Use this time to breathe. Connect to your five senses.

Intention: Numb

This is not a warm and fuzzy mantra, but I believe I'm entitled to feel numb today. I'm still in shock and everything feels surreal.

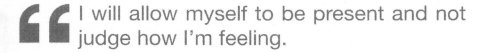 I will allow myself to be present and not judge how I'm feeling.

We might not understand why we go through these dark moments, and we have to come to a realization that we will never know why things happen the way they do.

Visualization

To be honest, I cannot visualize anything right now.

Everything looks black and formless. I feel like I am floating aimlessly with no direction. I visualize breathing.

That is all I can handle today, and that's okay.

Express Gratitude

Of course, I wanted more time with Jacob, but I am so grateful for those 18 glorious years with my son. I will cherish sweet memories of him. I will forever be grateful to God for gifting me with such an amazing young man. I am grateful Jacob had faith and that he will forever be whole, happy, and complete with God.

I am so sad the world didn't get to see him live up to his potential, but I do know he will forever be 18 years old in my heart. I am grateful I had the opportunity to be his mom.

Chapter 20 Waste Nothing

"Other people are going to find healing in your wounds.
Your greatest life messages and your most effective
ministry will come out of your deepest hurts."

RICK WARREN

A friend of mine messaged me about a dream she had with Jacob. She said he came to her in a dream and told her to tell us he was okay.

I focus and meditate on Jacob being okay. It isn't long until I realize that I am not thinking correctly. Of course, he is okay. The crazy thing is, he is more than okay! He is where we all long to be one day.

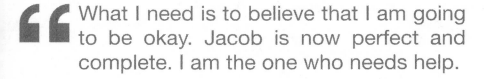

What I need is to believe that I am going to be okay. Jacob is now perfect and complete. I am the one who needs help.

I tell myself, "I am going to be okay."

I mutter this under my breath over and over until I can at least get out of bed. It doesn't work. I am still in bed, I haven't showered or brushed my teeth.

It's okay. I am going to be okay. I am lying in a dark room and I hear everyone outside the bedroom door. They are here visiting, bringing food, bringing hugs, bringing encouragement. But I cannot face anyone today.

I am grateful they are here to encourage us, but I just do not have it in me to face the world. I am not leaving this room. Maybe not ever. And that's okay.

I get a phone call from an organ donor organization. Erik does not have the emotional capacity to talk to them. I tell him it's okay, I'll do it. I spend the next 90 minutes answering questions.

I am numb and I disassociate. It is surreal to have this conversation about MY SON. Like, how is this even my reality right now!? The organ donor representative is full of compassion and grace.

She reminds me that there are many parts of the body that can still be useful. I answer her questions like I am answering some random survey over the phone. Except I am answering questions about my son's health.

I am shocked that I am not emotional at all when talking about which body parts they are interested in. I am totally not connected to the conversation.

She tells me that Jacob's corneas can be donated so people can see, his limbs for cancer patients who had to have their limbs amputated, skin grafts for burn victims, and so on.

At this point, I just say yes to everything. "Waste nothing," I think.

Somehow, talking to the organ representative gives me comfort. It is the only thing I accomplished today. I consider that a huge win for me. Jacob gave everything he had in this world and even in his death, he continues to give.

Thank you, Jacob.

G.I.V.E. Principle

Grounding

I breathe in new life-giving oxygen, exhaling out all that doesn't serve me. Experiencing death in such an intimate way, I begin to realize that I am not promised anything. The very breath that I take in is a gift and a miracle.

Jacob's death has me re-evaluating everything in my own life. I cannot tell you how many times I have said to myself, "I'll do it later... I have time... Maybe when..." Today I am determined not to waste anything.

Intention: Waste nothing

Today's intention has a defiant tone to it. I am determined not to waste my suffering. I repeat this mantra over and over again and I will make sure Jacob's story will not be wasted. I will continue to share his life, his legacy, his death to anyone who will listen.

Visualization

Jacob's organs can still help others in need and maybe my own suffering can help give others hope. I visualize sick people in need of these organs being able to use Jacob's body parts for their own healing.

I love to think that even in his death, Jacob is still serving others. And I visualize myself moving past this moment and eventually using it to help others in their times of crisis.

Express Gratitude

I am grateful I have a village around me taking care of me and my family. I am grateful that we are able to stay at our friend's house while they are away.

They made arrangements for their two youngest children to stay at a friend's home while we took some time to decompress and grieve as a family. Austin, Robby, and Robin's 20-year-old son, who was Jacob's childhood friend, stayed behind in case we needed anything. He is home from college and sacrificed his days just to be of service to us.

There is something about having his presence in the home that gives me reassurance. Almost like he was standing in for Jacob because God knows I am not ready to feel that vacant spot yet.

Chapter 21 Serendipity

"The coincidences or little miracles that happen every day
of your life are hints that the universe has much bigger
plans for you than you ever dreamed of for yourself."

DEEPAK CHOPRA

Erik and I are on our way to the funeral home to make
arrangements. The drive to Hollywood Hills is surreal. We sit in
silence and look out into space with blank stares. My mind feels
like a weakened dam holding back a flood during a massive
storm.

Memories rush in and I work on pushing them out for the time
being so I can keep my composure. My thoughts are
completely disjointed and random, just words and pictures
bouncing through my brain with no rhyme or reason. No thought
is complete, and few thoughts make sense.

All we can do is go through the motions and pray to make it
through today.

"We are looking for a plot and a casket for our eighteen-year-old
son." No parent should ever have to utter those words.

We meet with our funeral director; his name is Kanon. He has a
warm smile and a sweet disposition. He has excellent people
skills. I imagine that this job requires an incredible amount of
compassion and empathy. We can feel it emanate from his spirit
as he patiently answers all our questions.

As we walk to our private meeting room, we can hear another family behind closed doors wailing and screaming. Erik and I continue to walk through the hallway without any emotion. It feels like the *Twilight Zone*. I want to run out of here as fast as I can.

We sit and watch a short PowerPoint presentation and Kanon begins to describe all the available options. It is overwhelming to think about. We can't even process all that he is saying.

Shortly after, we drive around Forest Lawn cemetery to see which plots are still available. When we get to the top of the hill, Kanon tells us that they are building more plots on the other side because they are running out of space. My husband blurts out, "Wow! I bet people are really dying to get in here!"

Kanon looks at me to see if he should laugh or not and I just shake my head in disbelief. I tell Erik, "Too soon, honey, too soon." That broke the ice and released some of the pressure as we continued to look at plots.

When we find the spot, it is clear to us that this is where Jacob is supposed to be. It is perfect. The spot is overlooking Hollywood and right under a tree. We envision visiting Jacob with our family and having a picnic underneath the shade of that life-giving tree.

Next, we have to pick a casket. Who knew picking out a casket was like going to a car lot? There are so many choices to choose from. We start our search with looking at a super humble pine-wooden box to a gaudy, overly ornate golden casket for $30,000, and everything in between.

Kanon shows us the most basic and least expensive casket. It is an unfinished pine-wooden box with a Star of David on top. Erik and I are intrigued, and we ask a lot of questions about the traditions and theology behind it.

He explains to us that in the Jewish custom, they believe that you come from dust so you must return to dust. This casket is the most biodegradable of all the caskets. Before Kanon can show us another one, Erik and I look at each other and know this is the right one for Jacob.

We couldn't tell you why, but there is just this strong feeling we both feel to choose this casket. Kanon takes out his folder and walks closer to read the order number and write it down.

You could only imagine the shock and amazement we feel when we realize the casket was aptly named, "The Jacob." Wow! Are you kidding me!? How crazy is that!? The three of us stand there with jaws dropped to the floor in disbelief. We felt goosebumps all over. Serendipity!

So that's why that word came to me earlier today. Jacob is too funny. Well, that seals the deal. If we had any doubt at all, Jacob just confirmed our choice.

G.I.V.E. Principle

Grounding

In my practice, I use this time to connect to my spirit. A lot of people call it different things. Spirit Guide, Holy Spirit, intuition, gut instinct, little small voice within, whatever you call it, we all have it.

It is this sense of knowing. You can't put your finger on it. It is just a feeling you cannot deny.

So, today's word is serendipity. Interesting word to come up in the throes of my immense grief. I usually ask the Spirit several times if this is really the word He wants as my intention, and if He says "yes," I go with it even if I do not understand it.

Use this time to connect to your spirit. Breathe in surrender and trust, and exhale fear and anxiety. Continue to breathe through all five senses.

Intention: Serendipity

After my meditation practice today, I had to look up the word:

> **ser·en·dip·i·ty** /ˌserənˈdipədē/ *noun*: the occurrence and development of events by chance in a happy or beneficial way.

Today, I choose to look for the signs that Jacob is with us, communicating with us, and even in the afterlife, he continues to bring us joy and make us smile.

We love you Jacob!

Visualization

Today I visualize Jacob being with us. As we drive around Forest Lawn, I am convinced he is here helping us pick out the perfect spot for him. I know he also helped us pick out the perfect casket. He even made it extremely obvious so we wouldn't miss it!

I envision him being around us today. I feel his energy. I feel his presence. Today I visualize the beauty of *serendipity*.

Express Gratitude

Wow! I am so grateful for the way Jacob is showing us his presence today. The entire story about the casket is just so cool and very comforting. I love the signs that confirm that he's around us, guiding us.

I am grateful Erik and I had a great day. It was tough being at the funeral home, but Jacob made it fun and entertaining for us. I am grateful for our funeral director and how he made a very difficult experience a little more tolerable.

Chapter 22 Time Out

"You never know the true value of a moment
until it becomes a memory."

SPONGEBOB SQUAREPANTS

Earlier today, I was listening to people share their signs from
Jacob, whether from dreams or from cool coincidences. I was
feeling jealous because I wanted a sign too.

I began to meditate in the back of the Uber. After my
meditation, I asked Jacob. "Please give me a sign. I miss you
so much."

Before I finished my sentence, the song, "Good Riddance,"
from *Green Day* came on. This is one of Jacob's favorite songs.
Without a doubt, I knew that it was a sign. Thank you, Son.

Erik thought it would be a good idea for our family to get off the
grid and away from the hustle and bustle of the city before the
funeral and memorial services take place. We have been
through a lot and we desperately need a retreat. We need to
find a peaceful environment that will calm our minds.

Fortunately, my sister and her family live in the perfect place.
Marty's home is by a beautiful lake in the Seattle area,
surrounded by lush trees and wild nature. It is the ideal place to
decompress. We pack a few belongings, grab the girls;
including Jacob's girlfriend, Evelyn, who by now is part of our
family, and we head to Seattle.

We are so grateful to be all together as a family; no real agenda, no busy, hurried schedules; just a place to be still and enjoy the scenery.

I remember the last time we were here as a family. Jacob was with us. My brother-in-law taught Jacob how to ride a bike up here. We spent many Fourth of July's here, as well as Christmas holidays.

Their next-door neighbor Sierra came by and we reminisced about how when they were seven, Jacob tried to hold her hand when they were sitting on the dock. He might have even snuck a kiss in there.

In our winter visits we would build snowmen, open up presents at Christmas and just enjoy the carefree company of family. It is nice to be in a space where there are many good memories of Jacob.

It makes me sad at the same time to think about those memories. I miss those days.

The days where imagination led the way. The age where I can hear their belly laughs echo through the house full of joy and promise. The days before anxiety became Jacob's companion and pain pills his ineffective band aid. How I long for the innocence of that age.

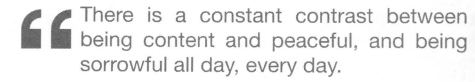 There is a constant contrast between being content and peaceful, and being sorrowful all day, every day.

G.I.V.E. Principle

Grounding

As you go through the breathing exercise imagine yourself in a peaceful surrounding. Remember that you always have access to this peace, even if you're in the middle of traffic, in the back of an Uber, or in your home with piles of laundry all around you.

Today as we breathe in and out, imagine yourself on a lake, or hiking up the trails and feeling the crisp chill in the air. Connect to all five senses with your breath.

Intention: Time out

As you walk through this difficult time of immense grief, allow yourself time to take a moment for yourself. Give yourself a time out. Get some sun, take a walk, get out in nature.

It is so important to pause and connect. Again, it is very tempting to isolate during this time out but if possible, get around people who love you and who love your loved one.

Visualization

Today, I allow myself to visualize every memory that surfaces. I can think of the summers spent here and the holidays we shared. I visualize every moment and hold it dear to my heart. I go through the memories as if they are in a photo album, and I am savoring each photo. I imagine what it would be like to have Jacob here now as a young man.

I know he would enjoy it. It would have been a nice break from the fast-paced life he was living in Hollywood.

Express Gratitude

Today I am grateful that our family is all together and enjoying the beautiful weather and view from the living room. We are looking out at the lake and the water looks like glass. It is so peaceful. No one is in the lake. No boats, no people, just the still lake inviting us to come in.

I am grateful for the much-needed family time and all the food we are enjoying with my sister's cooking. I am grateful for the time out. I will give myself permission to have as many time outs as needed.

Chapter 23 No Mistake

"Part of the journey is the end. What am I tripping for?
Everything is going to work out exactly the way
it's supposed to. I love you 3000."

TONY STARK, *Avengers: Endgame (2019)*

I had a special moment with my brother-in-law as we were sitting on their patio overlooking the lake. We were catching up and connecting over a cup of coffee.

I began to talk about all the would've, should've, and could've's with him. I started to second guess my decisions and actions. Only if we did…Only if we didn't…What if?… How did we not catch the severity of Jacob's addiction? How did the doctors and psychiatrists not catch it, either? How did all his friends not know?

As I lamented and rehearsed every scenario possible, Jim said plainly, "No mistakes."

He proceeded to share with me a story that Byron Katie tells in one of her books: *A Thousand Names for Joy*. Byron Katie is an American speaker and author who teaches a method of self-inquiry known as, "The Work of Byron Katie" You can find out about her methodology at: www.thework.com.

She talks about how soon after she 'woke up', people began coming to her home. When she answered the door, they would say, "Namaste." She thought, Wow, these people are so smart, because they keep saying, "No mistake."

Jim encouraged me to understand that there are no mistakes and we did everything we knew how to do. Something about the way he said it struck a chord and resonated.

I sobbed as I felt a physical release from the guilt and pain I was carrying. As a parent, it is nearly impossible not to blame yourself. After all, that was my one job, to love and protect my son. And I feel like I failed.

I loved him with every fiber of my being, yet he was still depressed. I protected him from every hurt I could see, yet he still sought solace in a pill. I knew I did all I could, yet it still wasn't enough.

Nothing I did changed the trajectory of his life.

I am grateful for this conversation. Jim reminds me that there are "no mistakes."

G.I.V.E. Principle

Grounding

Take a few deep cleansing breaths. Once your breaths are nice and deep, begin connecting to all five senses. With your eyes closed, move your eyeballs to the right, then to the left. Look up, look down. Feel the sensation of your eyeballs in your eye sockets.

Next, begin to look within and tap into your intuition and wisdom. Now, be mindful of your nose. As you inhale, be aware of what you are smelling. Maybe it is the aroma of freshly brewed coffee or maybe it is the smell of your morning breath if you haven't brushed your teeth yet. It's okay. No judgment. Just be aware of what you are smelling.

Now listen. What do you hear? Maybe it is some ambient noise, the refrigerator running, or the sound of traffic outside, or just silence.

Next is taste, what do you taste in your mouth? Maybe it is the remnants of toothpaste from this morning, or the after taste of your morning coffee. Bring awareness to your body and bring the breath to every inch inside of you.

Intention: No mistake

As I set my intention for my practice today, I remind myself that there are truly no mistakes.

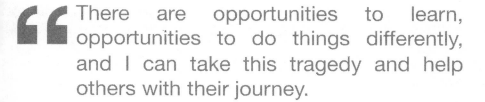 There are opportunities to learn, opportunities to do things differently, and I can take this tragedy and help others with their journey.

I choose to recite this mantra when doubts and guilt set in. No mistake.

Visualization

Today I visualize a time when I can feel peace without guilt and shame.

And it is with that knowledge that I can move forward - making new and better choices in the future. I visualize giving meaning to Jacob's journey.

I feel very passionate about bringing awareness to the opioid epidemic. It is a beast that must be fought head on!

I visualize an army of warriors going to battle to beat this monster that is destroying so many lives. There are too many parents in my situation feeling this unimaginable pain.

I visualize all of us standing together arm-in-arm. There is power in numbers, and we will fight to take back that power!

Express Gratitude

I am so grateful for my conversation with Jim today. I am grateful for the reassurance that there are no mistakes. I am grateful for his empathy and listening ear, not passing judgment or trying to fix something, but just being a safe place for me to process my feelings.

I am grateful to be able to release tears today. Tears are okay. They are proof you care deeply. I didn't know I had an unlimited supply of tears. I am grateful for the ability to be honest and raw in the moment. It is so freeing. I feel like a heavy load was lifted today.

Chapter 24 Do Something

"What we do in life echoes in eternity."

MARCUS AURELIUS

After my meditation, I immediately jump into writing my thoughts down before they disappear.

The words flow easily and keep flowing. I texted them to John, Jacob's business manager (who is also Jacob's uncle). I figured he could use the message to inform anyone who is interested in understanding what happened to Jacob.

We pack our bags, say our good-byes, and head back to Los Angeles.

By the time we return to L.A., John had finessed my words and turned my message into an article that was now being published on *Billboard* magazine! What!? I wasn't expecting that. But here it is...

From *Billboard* magazine:

> "June 24th was the day the neurologist came to inform us that my son's EEG results were not good. Jacob had been in a coma for eleven days. The doctor told us that, in the six days since Jacob's last test, he was starting to see a decline in my son's brain activity. The doctor was guarded, defensive and even angry to give us this news and to provide us further details. He definitely wasn't trying to sugarcoat anything. In his opinion, we had maybe a week left with our

son before he would be declared brain dead. With that declaration, the state of California dictates that a patient must be taken off of life support.

"I am very proud of how my husband, Erik, handled not only the news, but the doctor. Erik asked very pointed questions while, at the same time, trying to get the doctor's guard down. The doctor was combative. He repeatedly interrupted Erik and clearly didn't want the conversation to go on for long. Erik continued to be patient and kind, asking things like, 'How do you do this? Where do you get the strength to deliver this news? How do you prepare for this?'

"My husband's calm compassion eventually wore the man's guard down a little and he began to simply share with us. He was angry. Not at us, but at the impossible epidemic that is happening all around us. He said that he delivers this news to parents about once a week: Brain death due to accidental overdose or suicide. He was seriously upset and said, 'we' need to do something. By 'we' he meant that parents need to do something.

"I asked him, *What is the 'something?'* I hear this all the time; 'We' need to do something about mental health, depression, addiction, suicide, but *what is that 'something?'* He did not have an answer. Nor did the therapists, psychiatrists, in-treatment drug counselors, AA/NA sponsors, pastors, family, or anyone else who tried to help our son over the last two years.

"So, what is the 'something?' We feel it is a commitment to finding a way to confront the out-of-control distribution and use of Oxycontin and other opioids. We want the medical and recovery communities, the church and secular authorities, the government and health officials to come together and suggest a different way of triaging this everyday tragic event. Close down offending pharmaceutical companies and pharmacies, stop the ability to order these drugs online, put these easily available pharmaceuticals at the top of the enforcement list, change laws to give parents more options to oversee at-risk children after the age of 18, fund effective treatment and support; and stop blaming the parents, family and children most affected by this epidemic.

"That last one is important. You may not know it, but people you know at your church, your work, your school are quietly dealing with something like this and they are ashamed to talk about it. Opioids are incredibly addictive drugs that have taken the place of the can of beer, the joint, or whatever it was that some of us experimented with at that age. This is not a scare tactic. A friend of your child's', who does just as well in school, who comes from a family with the same social or economic status as you, will get their hands on these pills. It is not the family's fault, or the kids, or the teachers, churches, doctors, counselors, or friends who are all equally powerless against opioid addiction. We must protect our children now.

"We didn't get our week with Jacob. He died June 27th at 5:11 a.m. This is for Jacob. His life and death will count for something. This is our 'something.'"

G.I.V.E. Principle

Grounding

Breathe in, then exhale. Do this several times until you feel calm and subdued. Connect to all five senses.

I wake up with an intense and renewed energy. I haven't felt this alive in weeks. I wake up pissed off and determined. The devil picked the wrong momma to mess with!

I have to calm my breathing as my mind races feverishly.

I feel like I have an important message in my heart. I am tempted to hit the ground running, but I know I have to get grounded first. Breathe in, then exhale. I tell myself to do this several times until I feel calm and subdued. Connect to all five senses.

Intention: Do something!

I meditate on this mantra today. Do something! Action causes a reaction. I refuse to give up and feel sorry for myself. There is much to do, and I will do something to make sure Jacob's message is shared. I don't have to know the whole plan or have it figured out.

All I know is that I will do one thing daily toward making a difference in this world. Whether it's making a phone call, researching how to fight this opioid epidemic, or just reaching out to a grieving mom, I will do something.

Visualization

I visualize a movement coming together to fight for our children. As parents, we are the most important advocates for our kids. I visualize teaming up and helping to educate parents, teachers, leaders, politicians, law enforcement, thought leaders, church leaders, and anyone else who will listen about the dangers of addiction, the opioid epidemic, and mental illnesses connected to events like drug dependency.

I visualize an awakening. I visualize being able to be part of the solution before we lose more people to this devastating epidemic.

Express Gratitude

I am grateful for the platform I have been given. Obviously, the price is way too high, but nonetheless I will use it to bring awareness to the issue and to bring hope to this hurting world.

I am so grateful for the tools of *Grief Recovery* and for how these tools have helped me be present. I am grateful to be a resource to so many people struggling in silence and isolation.

I am grateful for the tenacity and resilience I have developed over the years to fuel me to make a difference.

Chapter 25 Awkward Silence

"The world is quiet here."

LEMONY SNICKET

My best friend Vicki (and her daughter Landry) picked up Emma and I from the airport in a limo graciously provided by our friend John. We were so grateful for the kind gesture. It was going to be a quick trip.

We landed early in the day and didn't know what to expect. I am a bit of a control freak and I am used to being the one who organizes events. This time, we were just asked to show up and I felt anxious about making sure the organizers had everything in place. 'Deep breaths' I thought…let it go.

The memorial was set to begin at 7:00PM.

A couple of hours before the event, I received a call from one of the young men putting together the memorial. He said, "So, what should we do tonight!?"

I began to panic! 'What do you mean what should we do tonight!?' My control freak antenna goes off as I get into my fix-it mode attitude….

Then I calmly asked him, "What is your vision for tonight? What would you like to see happen?"

He said, "I just want to create a space where people can share their memories about Sketchy and say good-bye."

I told him that was perfect, and that I trusted his plan.

We arrived at Zilker Park on a beautiful summer night. The vastness of the cloudless blue skies looked picturesque. I was struck by the vibrant green fields filled with people and dogs running around that contradicted the feelings of grey I had in my soul.

As we approached the west end of the park, we could see Jacob's friends plugging in the sound system and lighting the candles surrounding my beautiful boy's framed picture. I hugged every single one of them and we wept together.

I have gotten to know most of these artists and musicians through social media. I am used to their larger than life personas. Here. Now. Together, these kids were respectful, kind, and truly broken over the fact that Jacob was gone.

As the guests began to gather, there were people from school, church, the music scene, and fans who wanted to say good-bye. It was very healing to give real hugs to my friends who I hadn't seen since we moved to Arizona.

One of the organizers opened the evening by asking people to come up and share their thoughts about Jacob. At this point, there were probably about 200 people surrounding the makeshift memorial.

As I looked around, I saw somber faces, subtly lit by the candles they were carrying.

No one came up to the mic and there was an awkward silence that felt like an eternity.

It dawned on me that this was exactly what was needed.

It was perfect.

> You see, this generation doesn't know what to do with silence. When we have devices all around us to occupy every single second, it is fitting for us to just sit in it for a while.

The silence was needed to reflect on a life lost due to the senseless use of drugs that seemed to fill the void in the moment, only to create a bigger void when the high wore off.

If only Jacob knew how to fill that awkward silence and void.

I regret that he did not get around to learning this important skill in life. How to be comfortable in your own skin and be okay with the silence.

One brave soul got up to share and started the ball rolling...and then many people followed to pay their respects. Those kids impressed me so much. Their eloquence and wisdom helped me to have faith that this next generation is paying attention. They had a lot to share and they were truly broken hearted by losing Jacob.

We ended the night by playing Jacob's song, "Spent a Check," with all of us singing along. Jacob would want us to be happy. He spent his life making sure everyone else was happy, even though he never found that happiness for himself.

G.I.V.E. Principle

Grounding

It is time to connect to all five senses. Be present and be grounded. It is early and Emma and I are headed to Austin, Texas, for a memorial service for Jacob. The coolest thing is that this memorial service was initiated by some of the kids Jacob made music with. These young men took it upon themselves to organize a memorial so that Jacob could get a proper send off.

Hella Sketchy, the artist, was birthed in Austin. Jacob made many connections and his music started there.

I need to collect my thoughts and get grounded. Today is going to be an emotional day. Breathe in and out. I will take as much time as I need. Connect to all five senses.

Intention: Awkward silence

I love this intention. It is so important to create space for grievers to be awkward, to be silent, to be uncomfortable. I don't have to have all the answers. We can be still and be patient. This is perfect for today. Be okay with silence.

Visualization

I visualize Jacob being there at the memorial, probably embarrassed at all the attention and fuss he is getting. At one point, after one of the parents finished sharing a story, a brisk wind suddenly came out of nowhere and snuffed out the candles. Jacob's framed picture fell forward and cracked the glass.

I imagine that is Jacob saying, "Alright, that's enough. Move along, nothing to see here."

I look around and the vision of all the people my beautiful boy impacted with his short life warms my heart. He is loved and he inspires so many of his friends to pursue their dreams. Jacob wants everyone to win. He has never been competitive, at all. I know he is so proud of all of us.

Express Gratitude

I am grateful for our Austin community. We are so overwhelmed by the support. The level of love and encouragement is truly humbling. The next day we have a brunch at our best friend's home.

People come to share their condolences. We need a witness to our grief. Healing happens in a community of safe people with a shared experience.

We weep together.

There are so many families here who knew Jacob as a kid and our children grew up together and played together.

In a way, it hit us so hard because Jacob represents all parents' sons. If this could happen to Jacob, in a close-knit, loving community, then it makes us feel vulnerable that this could happen to anyone.

I am grateful for the love and the memories of our life in Austin.

Chapter 26 Be Present

"Most humans are never fully present in the now, because
unconsciously they believe that the next moment must
be more important than this one. But then you miss
your whole life, which is never not now."

ECKHART TOLLE

I wake up and immediately feel suffocated. I hold my breath to
try and keep my emotions from breaking loose.

My body is tense, my stomach is in knots. I sit up in bed and
stare at the clothes hanging on the door. I name three other
items in the room to bring me back. There is a glass of water on
the bedside table, a beautiful armoire directly across from me,
and the clothes I am going to wear to my son's funeral today.

I continue to ground myself to be present when all I want to do
is disappear. Slowly, I take a breath in and close my eyes. I
mutter to myself I am not sure how I am going to get through
today. I force myself to stay grounded and connected.

With each breath I loosen the tension, still my body, and relax
my shoulders. I stare at the clothes again, maybe if they
disappear, then this would all just be a cruel nightmare and I
can go back to reality.

But to no avail; the clothes don't move.

Today we have an intimate gathering of close friends and family to pay their last respects. Jacob will be buried in his wooden casket, appropriately named "The Jacob" and buried up in the Hollywood Hills with a beautiful view of the city.

Later, we will have a memorial for everyone to attend, but this first one is meant for those closest to Jacob and our family. We have an open casket viewing and I am comforted to know that his friend, Jackie, did his hair and make-up.

I am grateful that he has been prepared by loving hands from someone who knows him and cares for him. We arrive at the chapel and I immediately go to the casket to see him. I look at my beautiful boy laying so peacefully in the plain wooden casket.

There he is, bright pink hair, Fendi sweater, *Sex Pistols* T-shirt, graced with all his bling laying in the humblest of caskets. It is perfectly Jacob. He looks so good. He looks like he is peacefully sleeping. I cannot stop staring at him. I cannot believe that this moment is finally here.

This is not a sight I ever imagined.

My chest starts to burn, and I am starting to feel panic creeping its way in. "Just breathe," I tell myself. I focus my mindfulness breathing and stay present. As much as I want to run away, I have to be here, and I have to face this heartbreaking day.

It is a beautiful ceremony. Steve officiates the funeral and shares fond memories of Jacob as a child. Steve has been in our lives since before Jacob was born. People step forward and share so many heartfelt stories of how Jacob impacted their lives. I am so encouraged and proud of everyone who is sharing their heartfelt condolences, sweet memories, and funny stories.

Some of his friends can't get through their speech, and my heart aches along with them. It is a beautiful display of authenticity and I am in awe of how these young men articulate themselves so beautifully. The people who share their stories are a mixture of childhood friends and musician friends.

After all the stories and words by others, there is an open-casket viewing. Erik and I are at the end of the procession. As I see people in front of me weep and say good-bye, the finality of never seeing my son again sets in.

Seeing his lifeless body in the casket is agonizing. As I hold his hand and say good-bye, I wail, knowing that I will never, ever see him again in his physical form. It just tears my heart open.

Good-bye, sweet Jacob. Until we meet again, my love.

G.I.V.E. Principle

Grounding

It is time to connect to all five senses. Be present and be grounded.

I just breathe, letting the realization wash over me, "Yes, today is my child's funeral." I stare at it as if to remind myself that this is really happening.

I know my defense mechanism is to detach and disassociate. As a trauma survivor, this is a skill I have perfected since childhood. It would be easy to slip back into that habit.

> **But did I really want to cheat my son out of the last moments that we will physically be together?**

So little by little, with every breath, I come back to the room, to my physical surroundings. As I inhale, I come down to earth a little more. With every exhale, I release anxiety, fear, sadness, and despair. I sit up with clarity and make a conscious decision to connect to all five senses.

Intention: Be present

Today is an important day to be present. I am processing my grief not just day by day but moment by moment. I focus on taking one step in front of the other. I rely on those who have strength to carry me through today.

It's not easy but the only way out is through it. My mantra today is to repeat this over and over, "be present."

Visualization

Today, I visualize all the love that is in the room. There is an intimate group of about sixty people, and I can feel all the love. Jacob's peers amaze me. They love him so much and we all share stories of trying to help him with his addiction. It is evident that the people in that room all love him and tried their best.

I visualize Jacob being here, proud of all his accomplishments and especially proud of bringing all these people together and connecting all of us. My visualization comforts me.

Express Gratitude

Today I am so grateful to all the people who pitched in to make the funeral happen. So many people donated to our GoFundMe campaign with extremely generous donations. But what warms my heart are the countless kids who gave their last $5 to donate to Jacob. That meant so much to our family that these kids were willing to sacrifice for someone else.

The 60 or so people gathered for Jacob all enjoyed Panda Express and Cheez-Its, Jacob's favorite foods. It is a beautiful day to connect and express love and be there for one another.

I make it a point to share my gratitude with every guest that is here today. I will never forget you and the kindness you showed our family during such a devastating time.

You have helped me hold my head up high. I love you.

Chapter 27 Generosity

During our time in Los Angeles, a friend of mine was following our posts about our journey with Jacob. She is a medical professional and was so affected by the miraculous things that she was witnessing. According to what she has experienced firsthand none of this made any sense. As an ICU trauma nurse, she knew that the only way this was medically possible was God.

Every night, she was convinced it would be Jacob's last. She was amazed by the miracle of each post when she read that Jacob was still with us. She was so inspired and touched by our beautiful tragedy.

With tears in her eyes, Mindie told me that she hadn't prayed to God in a very long time, but Jacob changed that; she prayed for Jacob. She said that Jacob restored her faith in God again.

When I scrolled through social media, our posts were flooded with prayers from people all over the world. There are atheists praying. People from different beliefs and faiths. It is truly an incredible thing to witness.

In a time where we can have opinions about everything and argue online about the dumbest things, it is refreshing to see people come together for one purpose...to see Jacob healed.

When Mindie asked us if we would like to stay at her family's home while they were away on vacation, we accepted this unexpected invitation. Unbeknownst to us, they live in a mansion. And when I say mansion, it is a legit mansion! Basketball courts, eight-car garage, the guest house alone is 1,800 square feet! The house is amazing!

And even though nothing could fix our broken hearts, I guess if you're going to grieve, this is not a bad place to do it. There is a beautiful pool with a cascading waterfall, and I meditated there often. Those were precious moments I was fortunate to have in my time of grief. Evelyn, Emma, and I enjoyed our stay there.

Sadly, Erik had to get back to work and Sydney had summer camp. Again, I am beyond humbled by the generosity of Mindie and her family.

I am reminded of my many conversations with Jacob where we dreamed about where he would tour, the places he wanted to visit, and the mansion he was going to buy me. In a weird way, I guess he kept his promise. Thanks bud.

G.I.V.E. Principle

Grounding

Today I wake up and once again experience the now-familiar gut punch of grief that greets me every morning when I open my eyes. I reflect on the mantra today: Generosity.

Yesterday, I heard that word repeatedly as people shared their stories about Jacob. Generosity. Story after story, that is how his friends and supporters described him. Jacob was generous with his time, his resources, his money, his food, everything! I am so inspired and want to be more like him.

This mindfulness practice focuses on ways we can be generous today. Breathe in deeply, then exhale all the breath out of your mouth. Connect to all five senses.

Intention: Generosity

For today's mantra, I focus on the word, "Generosity." I look to Jacob and I am inspired to follow his example. I am also inspired by Mindie's family and the way they blessed us in our time of sorrow.

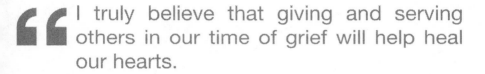 I truly believe that giving and serving others in our time of grief will help heal our hearts.

Visualization

I visualize Jacob being with us at the mansion. I know he would have enjoyed it. We share stories, home-cooked meals, hang out by the pool, and chill in the jacuzzi. We imagine he is there with us. And I believe he most definitely is.

One of the days we were there, we came upon a trail of pink bougainvillea petals in a straight line leading to the sliding-door entrance. Evelyn kept asking us who did that. Emma and I said it wasn't us. Then we knew Jacob was once again leaving us signs. I love my beautiful boy.

Express Gratitude

Today I am so grateful for our friend's generosity. It is nice to feel spoiled like we are hanging out in our own resort. I am grateful I have a beautiful space to meditate and unwind. I am grateful for their kindness. There are no words for how lucky I feel to have this opportunity to be here, away from the stress of life.

Chapter 28 Extra Grace Is Needed

"Make allowance for each other's faults and forgive
anyone who offends you. Remember, the Lord
forgave you, so you must forgive others."

COLOSSIANS 3:13 NLT

Today I notice I have a short fuse. I am agitated at everything,
and I am feeling irritated at the circumstances, no matter how
big or small. I find myself being annoyed at the outcome of silly
little things...and sometimes I even get mad at Jacob.

This is our mantra at home: "Extra Grace Is Needed." Our family
is grieving and when we are grieving, we are hurting; when we
are hurting, sometimes it spills out.

You've heard the saying, "Hurt people, hurt people." That's
because people who are hurting will hurt others along the way.
Today there is tension in our house and our family is having a
hard time getting along and processing our grief. We are all
handling grief in our own unique way.

Patience is running low and the atmosphere is getting a little
tense. Erik and I have agreed that when we get impatient with
one another, we will try not to take it personally. It is just grief.

Self-awareness is really important in times like this. I am being
more careful not to react, but to respond with grace. I do not do
it right all the time.

Frankly, I am the biggest offender.

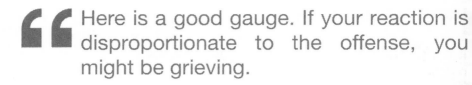

Here is a good gauge. If your reaction is disproportionate to the offense, you might be grieving.

For example, you are in the kitchen and you drop a plate. If your reaction is to have a fit, yell, scream, and cry...*you might be grieving*. If someone cuts you off while you're driving, and you respond with full-on road rage...*you might be grieving*.

Try to be self-aware enough to let your loved ones know that you might need some extra grace during your time of grief. Humility is required in communicating that you need a little bit of space or that you are just feeling sad and upset. Let that be okay.

Let's create a safe place in our home. Try not to take things personally. Let's really listen and take care of one another. Most importantly, let's practice self care and give ourselves as much grace as we need.

G.I.V.E. Principle

Grounding

During this season, expect to have a shorter fuse. As you go through your practice today, be aware of the ways in which you have been edgy, harsh, or a little impatient. It's okay. It is totally understandable.

Self-awareness is key. Understanding your triggers will help you have extra grace for yourself. As you release your breath, give yourself grace, ask for forgiveness where you need it, and start fresh with every new breath.

Let go of anything and everything that doesn't serve you well today. Breathe and connect to all five senses.

Intention: Extra grace is needed

It is normal and understandable to feel a little on edge in times of grief. Practice extending grace to others, especially the ones closest to you; but most importantly, have grace on yourself.

You are navigating a new season of life. It's going to take a minute to adjust. Allow yourself the grace not to be perfect. Let your loved ones know when you're having a hard day and ask for their grace.

Visualization

Today, I visualize a happy family with everyone getting along and showing kindness to each other. I visualize all of us being humble and vulnerable and having those safe conversations, sharing our deepest thoughts and feelings. I envision unity, laughter, and working together to make a difference in this world.

Whether it is through opioid awareness or just encouraging others, I pray we can do that as a family.

Express Gratitude

I am grateful for our family. I am grateful we can communicate and share our feelings, even when it is difficult. I love that we can talk about giving each other extra grace and then following through with that promise. I am grateful that, even though we are not perfect, we have been given incredible tools to communicate and connect.

I love how much we loved Jacob in our own way. We all miss him dearly. I am grateful that when Jacob passed, we all had the opportunity to have beautiful interactions with him. We are blessed to know that in our relationships with him, there was restoration and reconciliation.

Finally, what I learned in *Grief Recovery* is that unresolved grief is about undelivered communications of an emotional nature. The more you deliver your communication without fear of judgment or attack, the better you will feel.

Grief is energy, if you do not let it out, it will manifest itself in other ways that might not be beneficial to you. That energy will either implode or explode. I am grateful that all of us were able to share our hearts with Jacob.

Chapter 29 Just Keep Swimming

"Just keep swimming. Just keep swimming, swimming, swimming. What do we do? We swim, swim."

DORI, *Finding Nemo (2003)*

The nights and mornings are the worst. During the day, I can find things to keep me busy. There are a lot of planning and tasks to do. But when everything slows down, the avalanche of pain sweeps over my body and stops me in my tracks. I just can't. I miss my son. I want to hold him. I need balm for my soul.

This is what I read today:

> **The LORD bless you, and keep you [protect you, sustain you, and guard you]; The LORD make His face shine upon you [with favor], And be gracious to you [surrounding you with loving kindness]; The LORD lifts up His countenance (face) upon you [with divine approval], And gives you peace and a tranquil life and heart.**
> NUMBERS 6:24-26 AMP

I know there will be many days like this. I just have to keep swimming.

I saw a saying online that said, "When you're not struggling, you float."

It reminded me of something I heard at a lecture about our response to trauma and tragedy. We will either fight, flee, or freeze.

As a trauma survivor, this resonates with me. When I was younger, I fought a lot. I was angry and I lashed out at everyone. I had so much pain and I did not know how to process it.

As I have shared, I also became really good at fleeing, running away from my problems, and not dealing with any of it. I ran to drugs, alcohol, men, shopping, food, you name it, I did it!

I also experienced what it is like to just freeze, to be paralyzed with fear and do nothing. I struggled for years with not having good boundaries, and I did not honor myself. Frankly, I did not know how.

All of us know that these are unhealthy coping skills. I am learning to align myself with swimming with the current instead of feeling like I am always trying to swim against it. The idea of surrender used to be scary to me because I do not like to lose.

To me, surrendering means losing. That could not be further from the truth. I just did not understand the true meaning of surrender.

To surrender means to float, to be carried and to trust that God's got you. He will guide you and lead you. To surrender actually means you win, because you are no longer trying to do this life on your own.

The creator of the universe wants to help you and hold you close. Let Him carry you. He is for you.

G.I.V.E. Principle

Grounding

Today as you bring awareness to your body, imagine yourself swimming. Imagine floating and feeling a sense of peace. Start with a nice big inhale, then exhale. Go a little deeper with each inhale, and as you exhale, float a little farther out to the middle of the ocean where the waters are peaceful. Just float.

You are not fighting the current, today you are going with the flow. Now connect to your sight, what do you see? Your ears, what do you hear surrounding you? Your taste, do you taste this morning's coffee or breakfast?

The purpose of this grounding exercise is to get you to slow down and notice the senses we often take for granted because we're not paying attention.

Intention: Just keep swimming

I borrowed this mantra from Dori from the movie, *Finding Nemo*. She says this often in the movie and it has stuck with me. The idea of taking baby steps, and just swimming through this pain is very good advice.

The best thing we can do as we navigate this new path is to keep moving and keep taking consistent action. It can be as small as taking a shower or going to work. Celebrate the victories no matter how small they are. Showing up every day is very brave of you. Acknowledge that and feel proud.

Visualization

Today I visualize myself moving forward. Putting one foot in front of the other. I envision myself living my life and doing it for Jacob. He would want that.

As a grieving mom, I imagine myself digging a grave for my son, I have a choice whether or not to join him. My pain is unfathomable, it runs through my entire physical being and I feel like I cannot go on.

I have a choice. I can either die inside with him while I live my life as an empty shell, or I can choose to keep going and carry his message, sharing it with whoever will listen. I imagine my son cheering me on and encouraging me.

I will do this for you. I know you are gone and have moved on, but I am still here and every day that I still have breath in my lungs, I know I am not done here yet.

Express Gratitude

I am grateful for the moments of grief. I really am. It is a reminder of how much I love my son. I am grateful I have my health, my family, my job, and my community.

It feels wrong to be grateful when I am in so much pain, but I shift my energy and perspective to move forward. Just one step.

I just keep swimming.

Chapter 30 Fulfillment

"The quality, not the longevity, of one's life
is what is important."

MARTIN LUTHER KING, JR.

As you have read through this journal, you know that I always ask my Spirit to give me the Intention word for the day. My word for today is *fulfillment*. This word is fitting since today is Jacob's memorial. We get to celebrate a life that Jacob fulfilled.

As I began preparing for Jacob's memorial service, I had an overwhelming sense of peace, knowing my son fulfilled his mission in his short eighteen years on Earth. Jacob accomplished everything he wanted to do. He lived his life on his own terms, and he did so unapologetically.

This is what I shared...

"Thank you for joining us in this celebration today. We are so grateful for the outpouring of love and support and the incredible generosity. Thank you to everyone who has walked alongside us during this very difficult time.

"I want to share with you the kind of kid Jacob was. He was about three or four when he participated in his first Easter egg hunt. We were at a park, staring at hundreds of eggs all over the grassy field. All the kids there were so excited as they counted it down. 3, 2, 1. GO!!! Simultaneously, they all ran out and started clamoring for the eggs.

"Jacob walked to the first egg he came upon, picked it up, and put it in his basket. Then he started picking up eggs and putting them in other kids' baskets! Now I am Asian, I am a tiger mom, I like to win! I ran out on the field and was like 'Oh, no, no, no! This is not how this works. The one with the most eggs wins!' But Jacob didn't care. There was not one competitive bone in his body.

"Jacob's giving spirit never stopped. In this music industry where it is all about clout and who gets the most plays, likes, and all other forms of social adulation, Jacob did not care about any of it.

"He genuinely loved seeing his friends succeed. He was so proud of them and encouraged them. I was always amazed by that. Like for real, behind closed doors, he was truly happy for his friends' and peers' successes.

"When it came to fans, Jacob hated that word fans. He truly considered his "fans" his friends. It is evident by the way they speak about him. I have gotten countless direct messages and emails about how Jacob was their BEST friend! How many best friends did this kid have!?! It speaks volumes to how he made each person who came into his life feel special, no matter who they were.

"Last time we saw Jacob was right here at Mosaic in Hollywood. We heard pastor Erwin together, then had dinner at Panda Express. He could eat orange chicken all day long! Jacob wrestled a lot with his faith and what he believed, and how to live in this music industry with faith. He was hurting and vulnerable, and yet continued to love and believe in people. I know he loved God deeply but struggled with how to navigate that in his new world of being an artist in Hollywood.

"I am very proud of my son. Not because he accomplished

so much in his short life, but because of how he affected so many lives. So many emails poured in, with stories of how Jacob believed in them and inspired them not just with their art, but life stuff, even to the point of helping save kids from suicide.

"Jacob's heart was so big. Unfortunately, because it was so big and so deep, it was impossible for him to receive love for himself from those around him. His love was selfless.

"I wish everyone was like Jacob, the kind of friend who is nice to others. To be that kind of friend, you must go the extra mile. If you see someone struggling, get help. Get help for your friends.

"We are all in this together. Our family is here, ready for you. We want to be that safe place. We love you all. Energy never dies, it just redirects. Let's direct Jacob's energy in truly loving one another.

"One of the things I will miss most about Jacob is all the times he reached out to me... all the unsolicited texts, phone calls, and FaceTime. The ones he initiated were really special because when he moved out, I wanted to give him space, not smother him too much. I will miss those texts that simply said, 'I love you mom, I am thinking about you.'

"Please text or call your mother today. There is nothing like a mother's love. If you do not have a mom, feel free to message me: 512-897-5487. I can use all the love I can get!"

I really didn't think about giving out my number on the Internet, it just happened in the moment!

What I thought was a mistake turned out to become an incredible blessing!

I received hundreds of text messages with words of encouragement and stories about Jacob. I continue to get them to this day.

As I end my day today, I look back at my intention and the word *fulfillment* comes to mind. I think about what the scripture says...

> ❝ You have decided the length of our lives. You know how many months we will live, and we are not given a minute longer.
> JOB 14:5 NLT

I believe that Jacob fulfilled his calling on this Earth. From the day he was born, he set out to do what he did, and now it is up to us to continue his legacy. Believe in one another, inspire one another, and continue to encourage people to never give up on their dreams.

G.I.V.E. Principle

Grounding

As you inhale, think about how fulfilled you feel. As you exhale, think about all the reasons why you don't feel fulfilled. Is it fear, anxiety, not feeling like you are ready, afraid of failing, fear of failing someone you love? Take a moment to give it consideration.

Really think. As you begin to breathe through each of the five senses, think about each breath and focus on fulfilling each inhale and exhale.

Intention: Fulfillment

I love that this word was what I set my intention on for the day.

When I think about Jacob fulfilling his purpose on this Earth, I feel inspired and full of pride for what he has accomplished. I focus on the good things he left behind knowing that he has left an incredible legacy to encourage so many people with his art and talent.

When I think of him fulfilling his dreams, it brings a smile to my heart. Don't get me wrong, it is incredibly painful for me not to see MY dreams for him fulfilled, but I do believe he finished his race on his own terms.

Visualization

I visualize Jacob watching his memorial with so much pride. I am sure he would have been so amazed by a standing-room-only event! People from all over have come to pay their respects.

I envision him feeling all our love and realizing that he is such an important part of all of our lives. I imagine him with a huge smile on his face to see the outpouring of love and support. We are going to miss you so much. We will never forget you.

LLHS! (Long Live Hella Sketchy!)

Express Gratitude

I am so grateful for the way everything has come together for the memorial. There are so many people helping and coordinating. I am so grateful to all the people who are sharing their hearts. Thank you for your courage and vulnerability.

Thank you, Mosaic in Hollywood, for hosting an amazing memorial for Jacob with such grace and professionalism. We will never forget your kindness. Thank you to all the people who volunteered their time to serve.

We are so grateful for our friends: The Hagadorn's, who flew in from Austin, Texas. Chuck, Zach, and Cameron, who drove from Arizona. We have been reunited with so many people we haven't seen in a long time.

Although the circumstances are not what we would have hoped, it has been a beautiful display of love and honor for our son.

Chapter 31 Authenticity

"Today you are you! That is truer than true! There is
no one alive who is you-er than you!"

DR. SEUSS

Grievers are courageous. To be able to get up and face the
world in the midst of their pain takes nothing but courage. It
takes courage to show up in your life and speak your truth.

Authenticity is so freeing because you don't have to muster up
energy to be real.

Today, I choose to be courageous. I will get up, and show up,
and live my best life for Jacob. I will simply be authentic in my
feelings and courageous in my actions.

Part of my healing process has been to feel my feelings 100%,
without trying to mask them. I cry wherever and whenever I
need to. I also don't feel guilty for having joy. I stay present and
in this moment; I welcome it.

I will get up, and show up, and live my best life for Jacob.

A beautiful thing about being authentic is that it gives others
permission to be authentic too. I am very open and that
openness breeds openness in others.

I cannot tell you how many parking lots I have cried in, talking to
strangers and sharing our lives.

❝❝ Grief needs a witness. When we show up for one another and are real with one another, we realize we are not alone.

One of my favorite quotes is from C. S. Lewis: "Friendship is born at that moment when one person says to another: "What!? You too? I thought I was the only one!"

G.I.V.E. Principle

Grounding

Check in with yourself this morning. Start to bring awareness to your body with your breath. What are you feeling right now? What areas of your body feel a little tense? Are you experiencing physical pain? Our bodies will hold trauma and grief, it is important to release as much energy as possible.

Working out, yoga, hiking, walking, dancing, weight-lifting, are a few ways. Crying is also an important part of releasing energy from the body. Once you feel calm, begin breathing through your five senses.

Intention: Authenticity

Your greatest strength also has a corresponding weakness. I have always tried to live my life as authentic as possible. The flip side to that is that I have a hard time being fake. I have to get everything off my chest and sometimes it's not pretty, it doesn't come out right, and I hurt feelings along the way.

I am learning to have discernment and speak the truth lovingly. One of the questions I ask myself, "does my inside match my outside?" How is my self-integrity? What am I doing when no one is watching? These are hard questions.

The good news is that when you are truly living authentically, you can go to bed at night knowing you gave it your all and you held nothing back.

Visualization

I visualize myself being 100% present and thoroughly living my life to the fullest. My son has lost his life, but I did not lose mine, even though most days it feels like I have. I envision myself having a disciplined schedule, working out, eating well, volunteering, using my counseling skills to help people, and having the courage to live out my dreams.

Express Gratitude

I am so grateful for the many examples of courageous men and women who inspire me daily to show up and live my life fully. After giving out my phone number at Jacob's memorial, I have received hundreds of text messages, voicemails, and direct messages from Jacob's supporters.

The level of *authenticity* they have displayed is so inspiring. I am grateful to connect with so many young people who love Jacob and are touched by his music. Their honesty and courage humbles me. These young adults are so brave to share their lives with me.

Some of them come from challenging backgrounds and I can feel their pain. Others, like Jacob, come from spiritual homes, and still struggle with a lot of the same things Jacob did. I am grateful to connect to his tribe because it makes me feel closer to him.

I lost my child, but I gained a gigantic family worldwide.

Chapter 32
Everything Happens For A Reason

"Not everything happens for a reason.
Sometimes life just sucks."

ALEXA CHUNG

On this day I received a rather long, but exciting text from a woman I never met. Her name is Carol and she is Jacklyn's mom. Jacklyn is Evelyn's friend and was at the apartment and helped give Jacob CPR before the ambulance got there.

Here is what she wrote:

"So, as I sang the HU song (to learn more about the meaning of HU check it out here **www.Husong.org**), and directed my thoughts and words to Jacob, I fell asleep. I had a dream.

"Now mind you I never met Jacob. I just knew he was a friend of my daughter Jacklyn and Evelyn's boyfriend.

"In my dream, which was more of a true soul body visit, I see this tall, lean, young boy just filled with sweetness beaming out of him. He had a great big smile and the cutest dimples. He took my hand as if to let me know with total assurance that it was him.

"He placed my hand on his heart and said to me, 'Don't worry, I will open the doorway for you to talk to my mom that

I love so much. She's very caring like you are to your daughter Jacklyn.'

"And then I recall asking him, 'But Jacob I don't even know your last name?'

"He smiled, kind of like a real smart knowing type of smile and said, 'I have the HU built in my name from birth!!!'

"I was in shock at his awareness of the HU, like he had been living the HU his entire life! This is the true demonstration of love and how divine love truly is.

"Characteristics of living the HU:

- Kindness to all
- Treating all with love
- Being the real deal example of love and so much more!

"I said, 'Really Jacob you have the HU in your name!?! Wow!!! That's so beautiful! I am so blessed to know you. Even though I've never met you in the physical realm, now I am meeting you as a soul.'

"Then the most beautiful music and light show appeared as he walked into it and then he turned around and said, 'You know Carol this is really happening, and I promise I will make the opening for you to be in direct contact to my mom and give her this story and tell her I love her always.'

"Then he blew you and me a kiss with this hand gestures that he said you would recognize. He set off to the light and in a musical kind of synthesizer sound he said to me, 'I'll be back, look for me.'

"As soon as I woke up, I texted my daughter and said, 'I need to know Jacob's last name because he came to me in a dream and told me the HU is built in his name.'

"When she finally texted me back. I nearly fell over when she said it was 'THURESON!!!'

"I was like, 'I knew it! I knew Jacob had come for real!'

"It was way too real a message! I cried, with such joy, knowing what I always knew, that the soul is who we truly are!

"Jacob knew and lived his mission in life as he still does but he had a clear awareness of it. That made the big difference and he was so helpful to all the lives he touched.

"No doubt I knew him as a SOUL. So, then I kept asking my daughter to please tell me his stage name. She finally told me. I was having such trouble because the link (for the memorial) would not work and my daughter was too stressed to tell me anything or help me.

"So, I finally find out his stage name, Hella Sketchy and I googled it. I was proud of myself because I am NOT tech-savvy and I finally found the memorial.

"The crazy part was that I had no idea how I would ever reach you but Jacob assured me it would happen so you can imagine the look on my face when I watched the memorial finally early this morning and saw you share your phone number to contact you!

"I said 'wow! Jacob knew it!' but I never expected it like that! I was so excited to text you!!! You have no idea how much I was touched by your son Jacob as I never ever knew or met him in the physical realm, yet my heart was so much more opened by this whole experience and I know for sure that this was all meant to be, as God makes no mistakes, and all is in his divine order!!!

"I believe that we truly exist as a soul and spiritual being on this Earth and that is what we really are.

"So yes, as tough as it is when a young child passes on and people are shocked or saddened with grief, its true purpose is that their mission has been fulfilled as it may be to teach those left behind how to love. To come together more or bring deeper awareness on an issue such as with Jacob and the opioid epidemic to get more people to stop and get help."

WOW! I can't even.... how do I even process this!? I am actually laughing to myself because there's really no rational reason why I gave my phone number out at Jacob's memorial. Now I know why. Everything happens for a reason!

G.I.V.E. Principle

Grounding

As we begin our grounding-mindfulness practice today, you will practice and feel surrender. Surrender your breath, just give it up, and see how easily and generously God gives you new breath and new air.

Do this for several breaths. Now connect your breath to each of the five senses. Breathe deeper every time. You got this! I believe in you.

Intention: Everything happens for a reason

To be honest, this is one of those cliché statements people make that make me cringe. I don't like to offer this statement as a form of encouragement because frankly, it's not encouraging.

In this instance, I found it funny that I truly did give out my phone number for a reason. One of those reasons was so that Carol could contact me and share that beautiful dream.

I will never forget it.

Visualization

I loved this soul visit so much! I can just visualize Jacob and Carol talking. I can envision him still being a prankster even in the afterlife. I envision him coming to visit me and sharing with me all that he is experiencing. I imagine being able to hold him, hug him, and cry just seeing him.

Oh, how I miss you. Please visit me in my dreams.

Express Gratitude

I am so grateful for this text this morning. I am overwhelmed with joy by how God works. I am grateful Carol took the time to share her experience with me because it gave me comfort.

I am so happy to hear that my beautiful son wanted to give me a message of love. I am grateful for my relationship with Jacob.

He is definitely a special soul.

Chapter 33 I Am Angry

"There are two things a person should never be angry at,
what they can help, and what they cannot."

PLATO

I hope that by expressing my real, raw emotions it helps give you permission to feel your emotions at 100%!

There is no right or wrong way to feel our feelings. It is what it is.

I think a lot of time we tend to filter and tame what we are feeling because of what we perceive others may think is appropriate. Right now, give yourself permission to be real.

Good, bad, or ugly, it is what it is.

I am angry! This sucks! I am mad that Jacob isn't here, and I miss him. I am also mad at the really stupid choices he made to ruin his life, his potential, the pain he's caused his family and friends. I am mad at all the doctors and medical professionals who didn't take Jacob's condition seriously. I am mad that we didn't do enough to help him.

I am just really pissed off!

Today, we finally had the wherewithal to go through his unreleased music. We listened to roughly 100 unreleased songs. His record label thought we might want to listen to them. It was hard.

" There is no right or wrong way to feel our feelings. It is what it is.

It was hard to hear his voice, knowing that whatever is recorded is all that will ever be. His voice is finalized and immortalized.

It was hard to listen to his fun, infectious energy and witty lyrics, my heart ached for that part of my son.

It was also hard and frustrating to listen to some songs with incredibly immoral lyrics, and especially the ones dealing with drug use. He wasn't hiding his usage. It was right there, recorded for everyone to hear. I hate it so much. It is not cool. It is not hip. It is nothing but destruction.

I couldn't bear to listen to it anymore.

Listening to his music took me back to when he was in the hospital hooked up to machines in a coma.

As friends, peers, colleagues, and recording industry guests came to visit, I remember taking them by the hand to show them the reality of the drug culture in Hip Hop.

I wanted them to take a hard look at what it really looks like to rap about lean (if you don't know what this is, you should), pills, and drugs. I wanted them to see the contrast of the glamorized music videos versus the reality of seeing Jacob in a coma fighting for his life.

I could tell it was hard for them, it was a sobering look at what this music culture is putting out there. I told these young and old creatives that they have a responsibility to what they are putting out there, people are watching, and whether you like it or not, you are a role model to kids all over the world.

We must be more conscientious about what kind of energy we are we putting out there. Not just in hip hop, but in general. Our words either speak life and positivity or death and destruction. Be aware of the impact you have on others. Words and actions matter.

To top it off, I was going through hospital bills. Hundreds and thousands of dollars in medical bills. And for what!? A waste of a gifted life. A life I gave birth to. A life that was my sweet child before he got engulfed in the flames of addiction. I am so mad today.

Mad at the circumstances, mad at Jacob, mad at the world, just mad! And I am mad at myself for being mad! I ate two chocolate bars and I surprisingly feel better. Thank you for letting me vent.

G.I.V.E. Principle

Grounding

Take a moment to bring awareness to your five senses. I have to breathe through the seething breaths. I am seeing red right now and my blood pressure is up.

It is the first time on this journey that I have given myself full permission to have another emotion other than just sadness. I am mad at the situation. I am mad that he is not here. I am mad that I am dealing with a pile of medical bills. I am mad that I've been on hold with the insurance company for what feels like forever.

I am mad that Jacob wasn't thinking about the aftermath and the pain this would cause.

As I breathe through the anger, my breath is getting calmer and my heart rate is going down a bit. I have to focus on things I can control. Some days, the only thing I have control over is my breath.

Take a moment to bring awareness to your five senses. Exhale out the anger and the fear. Inhale in the peace that transcends all understanding.

Intention: I am angry

As I meditate on this mantra, I allow myself to go there. We are taught what we should do or not do, feel or not feel. Anger is a natural emotion and it's okay to feel it.

It's not only okay to feel it, it's healthy to acknowledge these feelings and let it run its course.

So many times we suppress the "bad" feelings. Where do you think it's going to go!?

Bring your awareness to the emotions, notice it, feel it, breathe through it, then release it. It has served its purpose. Thank you.

As Phil Jackson said, "But trying to eliminate anger never works. The more you try to suppress it, the more likely it is to erupt later in a more virulent form. A better approach is to become as intimate as possible with how anger works on your mind and body so that you can transform its underlying energy into something productive."

Visualize

Today, I visualize peace. I need peace. I need to let go of my anger. I am angry at all the things that are beyond my control. I envision myself being so connected to my truth, being secure in who I am, and knowing that I did all I could to help save Jacob.

The truth is, even with my best effort, I could not save him. You cannot help someone who doesn't see their need for help. I don't have that much power and control. I need to release myself from that guilt and position. I visualize myself relaxed and not uptight. I visualize myself calm, cool, and collected.

I am full of peace and love.

Express Gratitude

I am grateful for the ability to express anger in a healthy and normal way. I am grateful for the tools that I have learned and the opportunity to learn life-changing programs that teach me how to have emotional intelligence and self-awareness.

Our human emotions are what make us unique. I am grateful I have a safe place to share my feelings. I know that feelings are not facts. But it's okay to honor what I am feeling, validate, investigate, then release and move on. I am grateful for the chocolates. That helped, too.

Chapter 34 Find Purpose For Your Pain

"Be patient and tough; someday this pain
will be useful to you."

OVID

Sometimes you find your purpose, then other times your purpose finds you. If you woke up today, I want to remind you that God is not done with you. You have a purpose. You were created with a calling on your life, to make a difference, to make an impact. You are still here to live fully for your loved ones.

No one wants to be part of this club and yet I have come to find out there is an army of us out there dealing with this nightmare, alone, isolated, and struggling in silence. If you are struggling with mental illness, addiction, depression, or other debilitating illnesses, I am here for you. No judgment.

My son happened to be a public figure, so there have been many keyboard warriors who never knew our family, professing their opinions on what we should have done.

One person tried to insult me but ended up giving me a compliment instead. After seeing me in the memorial video someone commented, "Look at her, she looks young and she has Hollywood hair. She probably didn't have time to be a good mom!"

I was flattered that this person thought I looked young and whatever Hollywood hair means, "Thank you!?"

Lots of people have blamed Jacob's upbringing for his addictions. Others blamed the industry or his 'friends.' It's okay.

For me, I am not going to shy away from this. I am not afraid. I will continue to shed light and keep the conversation going. I am willing to take the shots and be on the front lines. I will take the bullets, shame, and critiques if it means bringing light to this important topic.

I am on my way to the cemetery to visit my 18-year-old son's grave. This is reality.

As I drive, I am continually praying for God to give me supernatural strength. I creep up the road toward his plot, trying to focus on where I am and what I am doing. It is painfully hard. The road ends and I park the car. I take a few breaths before stepping out, then slowly make my way to where the grass had been newly placed. To see the earth and know that my son is buried underneath that dirt is sobering. I want to lay on the grass, and I want to be close to him. I want to see him one more time.

Nothing prepares a mother for this. I am glad I am not alone. It is nice to be with family and friends to walk through these tough storms together. We are not meant to go through these trials alone.

As I think about dirt, I think about how we started from dirt and how we return to dirt.

 We all have an expiration date. We don't know when our time is up.

When I struggle with my faith and start to question God and everything else, I am reminded that the Bible says all our days are numbered. God knows what our journey is going to be, whether long or short.

On this side of heaven, we will never understand the reason why life sometimes seems so unfair.

When I look to God and His word, I have to choose to believe His promises. He is good. He has a plan. As long as I am still here, and I have a pulse, He has a plan for me, and He is not done with me yet. If you woke up today, I encourage you to push through.

Find a purpose for your pain.

G.I.V.E. Principle

Grounding

Begin your breathing exercises. As you inhale, begin to bring awareness to your breath. Is it shallow, is it deep? Continue to go a little deeper and relax into your seat.

Remember, it is normal to be distracted or even irritated. You are disciplining your mind to take a few moments to be mindful of your breath and to focus on your mantra.

There is no judgment. Just be present. Begin to bring your breath to all five senses.

Intention: Find purpose for your pain

As I begin the mantra portion of my practice, I set my intention to this anthem, "Find Purpose for your Pain."

You have two choices. You will either ask the question "Why"? And let that question take you down on a downward spiral that you will never find an answer to, or you can ask "What"? What am I going to do with this pain?

I will find purpose to this pain. I have to.

It's moments like this when you begin to cultivate strength and resilience. It's moments like this when you want to give up but call out for strength instead just to make it through the day.

Keep showing up. Keep putting in the work. Keep putting one step in front of the other.

By the time you know it, you will surprise yourself. You will look back and be amazed at how far you've come. I know you don't feel it right now, but trust me, you will make it through.

You might be surprised to know that your pain is directly connected to your purpose. Don't waste it. *Use it to propel you forward*.

Visualization

Today I visualize the purpose for my life. Jacob lived 18 short years, but his purpose was clear, and his message and legacy is timeless. He lived his life fully and with no apologies. He made his art and vulnerably put it out there and paved his own path.

I want to follow his example of going all in and not leaving this world with my song still inside of me.

There's a video from Prince EA (you can find it here... **www.youtu.be/oKAmujgS4mo**) and he says the graveyard is the wealthiest place in the planet. All the songs never sung, books never written, relationships never reconciled, businesses and inventions never realized all because of fear, not feeling good enough, and not feeling worthy.

Now is the time, we are not promised tomorrow. Stop making excuses. Live today like it's your last. Use everything thrown your way towards your purpose and calling. Do it messy, do it scared, do it anyway.

Visualize what that looks likes for you. What can you accomplish if nothing was in your way? You can do this!

Express Gratitude

I am grateful for my newfound purpose. I now have a calling to share Jacob's story with the world. I pray that my efforts will help people seek help, feel heard, feel like they are not alone, and that somehow my story will give them strength. I am grateful for the ability to express myself in this way and my prayer is that it reaches all those who need it.

Chapter 35 Good-Bye For Now

"Don't cry because it's over. Smile because it happened."

DR. SEUSS

Today I say goodbye to L.A.! When I got here, on June 13th, my son was alive, fighting for his life. Today, I go home, and my son is gone. Forever.

I don't really know how to process this. I am sure it will take some time and there will be many layers to uncover. All I know is that I couldn't have done it without Robin.

She is the most loyal, loving, caring, sacrificial friend anyone can ask for. We invaded her home and have taken over their lives during this tragic time.

Erik is wondering when I am planning on coming home. He is already back to work in Arizona and Sydney is ready to go back to school.

To be honest, I don't want to go home.

I am scared.

I am scared to be back in our home without Jacob. I don't want to see his room. I don't want to face life without him.

For some reason, being in L.A. was encouraging for me. I was around all of Jacob's friends.

> **❝** I loved being around people who knew him. It helped me to connect and relate the deep pain we were all experiencing together; they got it.

I drove around areas where we had many happy memories together. I drove by our old house, the skatepark, the parks where Jacob played basketball, it was healing for me to be there.

Now I am going home. I have to face the inevitable. A piece of my heart will always be in L.A. Jacob is buried in Hollywood so I know this will always be his home.

Goodbye, for now, my love. Mom loves you so much!

G.I.V.E. Principle

Grounding

Every day on this journey I have to face the reality that Jacob is gone. It still feels so surreal. I want to forget and keep myself distracted, but the reality is, he is gone. I inhale good memories that make me smile, and I exhale goodbye to my son.

I focus on his energy. I focus on his energy still being around me, around his friends, and all who love him.

I breathe in all that positive energy and exhale out all the negative. Now, connect to all five senses.

Intention: Good-bye for now

Wherever you are today, even if it is just for this meditation portion of your day, make a conscious effort to say goodbye.

Maybe it's saying goodbye to a loved one, a relationship, a job, a city, a home, etc. Whatever it is, imagine letting it go, even if it's just for this short moment.

Now, investigate how you feel letting go of the extra weight you are carrying. What fears can you let go of here? What pain? What grief?

Little by little, give yourself permission to say goodbye. Take small steps towards your healing.

Visualization

I visualize all the places we used to frequent when Jacob was a child. I visualize him skating at the skatepark. I visualize him playing guitar with his band. I visualize all his childhood friends, all the sleepovers, all the amazing people we have connected with over the years. I visualize being able to go home to Arizona.

I imagine being able to be home and focus on the good memories of Jacob. I imagine being home, seeing his room, all the family photos, and being okay. I visualize being more than okay. I see myself able to face it with strength and grace.

Express Gratitude

I am grateful to the Noll family for adopting us and allowing us time to grieve in their home. Their friendship and generosity define the essence of human-kindness.

We are so grateful to the many people who showed up for us. It is truly remarkable and incredibly humbling. We have no words.

We are amazed at how everyone has come together to comfort us while celebrating our son's life. We feel so much love and support.

If you are reading this and you contributed financially, brought us a meal, said a prayer for us, or helped us in any way, shape, or form, thank you from the bottom of our hearts.

We will never forget you. Our lives are enriched by your love.

Chapter 36 Finding My New Normal

"Hope begins in the dark, the stubborn hope that if you just show up and try to do the right thing, the dawn will come. You wait and watch and work: you don't give up."

ANNE LAMOTT

My friends who have lost loved ones warned me that the days and months coming up were going to be the hardest. Now that all the busy-ness of planning a funeral and memorial are over, I must sit with my feelings and experience my new normal. It has been amazing to have so much support.

But eventually, everyone continues on with their lives.

I feel stuck, I feel paralyzed. I don't want this new world I am living in. I want to reject it. Close my eyes and wake up to a different reality. This one is too painful to bear. The pain is still so overwhelming that sometimes it literally stops me in my tracks.

At times, I could just sit and stare, trying not to feel, trying not to think, trying to just let time pass. It takes incredible willpower to move forward; for Jacob's sake, I persevere and not let his life be in vain.

What will my new normal look like? How will I ever feel whole again? There is no pain like a mother losing a child. Nothing I could ever have imagined. Now my eyes are opened to how many of us are walking around carrying this pain and devastation.

> **" "** I give myself permission to grieve at my pace. I am not going to rush myself.

I read a post and it explained that when a husband loses his wife, he is called a widower. When a wife loses her husband, she is called a widow. When children lose their parents, they are called orphans. There are no words in the English language that describe when parents lose their child.

There are no words because it is not supposed to happen that way.

It is not the right order of things. Yet, here we are, an army of parents, aimlessly wondering how we are ever going to find our new normal.

As I join many grief groups online and in person, I connect and bond with these families. When I look into a mother's eyes who has lost a child, we feel an instant connection with one another.

The more I learn about these groups, the more I am saddened to see how ill-equipped we are as a nation in handling grief. We must model this behavior with each other. Our tears, pain, and healing connect us to each another and our own healing journey helps heal others.

The idea that we are not alone in our grief brings lifesaving relief and hope. I hope I can do that for others, even in the midst of my own pain.

I often hear people say, "Wait until you are healed before you share your pain."

I respectfully disagree. When it comes to losing a child, you never heal. You just find a new normal. Eventually, my new normal will be my normal.

G.I.V.E. Principle

Grounding

Breathe in and exhale out. Begin to settle into your breath. Mindfulness means being completely in the moment. Mind, body, and spirit.

The best way to connect is just to breathe through all your five senses. Spend three to four breaths on each section.

Once you feel relaxed, begin to meditate on your intention today.

Intention: Finding my new normal

Try not to put too much expectation on yourself as you begin to integrate back into your life. Grief is very unpredictable and will knock you down without warning.

As I go through the early days of my grief, I allow myself as much time to heal. No judgment.

It is imperative that you begin a ritual of self care on your path to healing. The consistent practice will help you find balance and normalcy.

Maybe it's meditation, a walk, or a tranquil bath. Whatever it is, take the time to take care of yourself.

Visualization

I visualize what my new normal looks like. A day where my mind and heart won't be consumed by heartache and pain 24/7. I envision being able to laugh and enjoy my days without feeling guilty. I imagine being able to have good thoughts about Jacob and enjoy good memories.

I visualize our entire family connecting, enjoying one another, and being able to reminisce together about fun and happy memories.

Express Gratitude

I am grateful for the ability to practice self-care. Self-care should be high on the priority list for all grievers, and I am doing the best I can. I am giving myself grace.

I am grateful for the practice of meditation, mindfulness, therapy, yoga, Pilates, hiking, drinking water, and other activities to take care of myself. It has been a stressful last few years.

I have gained 20 pounds and I have struggled to get back to the discipline of my workouts. I know that should be the least of my worries, but being a health and wellness professional, I am going to have to stop eating my feelings.

Normally, this would put me into a deep depression and really mess with me and my self-worth and self-image. I am grateful for my strong mental health and that through the tears, I can still have a sense of humor.

Chapter 37 It's The Little Things

"You can become blind by seeing each day as a similar one. Each day is a different one, each day brings a miracle of its own. It's just a matter of paying attention to this miracle."

PAULO COELHO

As we go through our mantra today, I encourage you to remember all the little things.

It is the little things that could now easily bring me to my knees when I least expect it.

I was feeling completely out of sorts today, and this is what I posted:

"I miss folding Jacob's laundry. I miss clearing out 29 empty water bottles from his room. I miss his late-night post-mate deliveries from Pizza Hut. I miss hearing him play video games in his room. I miss the laughter. I miss listening to him make music in his bedroom. I miss the little things, just as much as the big things.

"The dreams about the tours he was going to go on. We talked about going to Japan and the Philippines. I will miss hearing about his new music. I will miss his banter and interaction with his sisters. I will miss seeing Jacob and his dad go to every new Marvel opening movie. I will miss everything."

" " It's kind of ironic that the things I used to get annoyed at are now things that I wish I could experience once again.

Grief is interesting. I get triggered by the most unexpected things. I went to Panda Express for dinner last night and it just wasn't the same. The other day I was at the grocery store and saw Cheez-Its. I was sad because I knew I would never buy another box. Only Jacob ate them.

Today, I thought I could clean out Jacob's room, but I couldn't even throw away his trash. This is so unlike me. I hate clutter and I like to keep things tidy. I can't explain it, like I wanted to keep everything as he had it so that I could envision him in his room.

He had an empty container of acne face wash in the bathroom and the sight of it just threw me to my knees, I bawled like a baby in my closet. Maybe it was the realization that he was only eighteen. He was just a pimply teenager that had his whole life ahead of him. This shouldn't be happening.

Grief comes at the most unexpected times. I roll with it. It is part of the process.

G.I.V.E. Principle

Grounding

Today as we focus our mindfulness practice, key in on feeling your entire heart. No judgment and no shame. Give yourself permission to feel whatever you are feeling today. Now breathe through those emotions.

If you are feeling anger, can you trace it back to grief? If you are feeling joy, do you feel guilt or shame?

It is time to own whatever you are feeling right here, right now. No apologies, no saying the "right" thing. Just connect the breath to the emotions.

Now as you go through the five senses, let it all go with every exhale. Let go of everything that does not serve you well today.

Intention: It's the little things

As you meditate on this mantra, allow yourself the time to remember good memories of your loved one.

Think about the little things…their laugh, their favorite food or movie, or whatever comes to mind.

If you still have their belongings, allow yourself the time to touch and hold their favorite shirt or stuffed animal. Find the connection to them in the little things. Don't try to hold it in. If you get emotional, don't stop the flow.

From the Grief Recovery Institute:

> "Did you know that tears of grief contain leucine enkephalin. A natural painkiller released when the body is stressed. So when you tell someone to stop crying, you are asking them to deny themselves natural pain relief."

Visualization

I visualize happy memories of Jacob's childhood. I realize even the annoying memories are now super special. I envision his laugh. He truly had the best laugh although his laughter was usually at the expense of pranking someone.

One time he took the cream out of an Oreo cookie and replaced it with toothpaste. He left it and then waited to see who was going to pick it up and eat it. I was the sucker!

I remember that laugh. I miss that laugh.

Express Gratitude

Today I am grateful that I have many beautiful memories to remember Jacob by. I am so grateful for all the times we spent together. I am so happy that at the time of his passing, our hearts were clear.

There was no animosity or unforgiveness between us. We had the best talks prior to his death. Jacob gave me the greatest gift. He told me I was the closest person in his life and that he felt safe telling me anything. I cried so hard.

I told him, "That's all I ever wanted was for us to have a close relationship."

And in true Jacob fashion he laughed and said, "Well, you got it Mom!"

Chapter 38 Signs And Wonders

"Miracles happen every day you just have to
look for them, they are there."

ANONYMOUS

Here are a few signs and wonders we have experienced...

*From Carol, the same mom who had a spiritual visit from Jacob in
her dream...*

"I am a singer for a big band show with 20 musicians. I kept
feeling Jacob's presence all around me as we rehearsed for
this show. During dress rehearsal I get a call that my lead
trumpet player is ill and can't make the rehearsals and the
show.

"We have been working on this show for a year and I start to
panic. I could not help but notice this incredible vibe coming
from Jacob. It was all around me and it was so
overwhelming!

"It is my responsibility to replace this musician, so I start to
make endless calls with no luck. I just keep trying my best
and each time I sit and surrender it, all I feel is Jacob all
around me and in a funny kind of way, like when the kids
were little and played hide and seek and tried to say, 'Hey
Mom, can you find me?'

"It brought a sweet distraction from the challenge I was
facing at this crucial time. Then the next thing I know I get a

text message from the musician that is ill that his friend's son is a musician but that he's only 18 years old and is a student.

"He reassured me that even though he is young, he has experience and can read music. I was nervous because we are all professionals and I have my head on the line here. I need a miracle!

"Then as I continue to feel Jacob's presence around me, the phone rings and I say, 'Hello?' He says, 'Hi, this is Jacob and I can do this show for you Carol.'

"'What? Jacob? Jacob who?'

"'Oh, I thought my dad told you about me. I am 18, a student, but I can read music and am available for your show.'

"I just stood there in awe with my jaw dropped to the ground.

"I got a new musician named Jacob and he had to be driven to my house to rehearse and escorted to the show by his parents who were so caring, sweet, helpful, and they were so supportive.

"I kept calling her Jacob's mom and she said, 'You don't have to call me Jacob's mom, my name is Judy.'

"'What?' I exclaimed!

"She said, 'Oh, I didn't mean to startle you, sorry. I just wanted you to know that you can call me Judy instead of Jacob's mom.'

"'Oh yes, okay!' Then I mumbled to myself, 'My goodness, Jacob, you really are a great soul. You are still here helping all that was needed to put the pieces of the puzzle together!'

"Thank you for the miracles and gifts of the spirit no matter what world we are in!"

From my friend Robin...

One afternoon when my friend, Robin, and I sat together on her back patio, she noticed that a yellow butterfly kept circling us. Evelyn called me while we were out back and shared that she just had a dream about a butterfly landing on her hand and it got stuck.

In her dream, she kept trying to release it, but it refused to fly away. When I asked her what color the butterfly was, she said, "Yellow."

From my friend Claire...

My friend Claire created my branding and logo for my new website and created a logo of a butterfly not knowing what the butterfly meant to me.

From my niece, Tani...

She went to the nail salon to get her nails done and wanted a pink color that matched Jacob's hair. When she found the perfect pink color, she looked at the number on the bottle and it was 1111.

Well, Jacob's birthday is 01/11/01, and when she looked at the name of the nail polish it said, "Happy Birthday."

From Jacob's memorial service...

At Jacob's memorial, Robin was one of the speakers. She remembered a story of when a group of the kids were on the trampoline in her backyard and a couple of the kids got into an argument. All the other kids were taking sides except Jacob.

He was determined to be the peacemaker. He refused to take sides and so he sat down in the middle of the trampoline, criss-cross-applesauce until the kids got their differences resolved.

About a week or so later, she found a picture on her desk of Jacob and the other kids on her trampoline. It was a picture from that very day she spoke about. All the kids were on the trampoline.

Next to the picture was a pack of Spider-Man temporary tattoos. Jacob loved Spider-Man. She asked everyone in her family how those items ended up on her desk. No one knows how it got there! It just appeared out of nowhere!

From Jacob...

Jacob's birthday is 01/11/01 so whenever I see 11:11 I think of him and I think it's his way of saying hello. Jacob is busy. I can't tell you how many people share their dreams with me.

Also, he must have a twin out there because people often tell me they see someone that reminds them of Jacob.

I love all the signs, dreams, wonders, and God-winks, it is a reminder that he is still all around us, watching us, and maybe even trolling us!

The last week of editing the book, I was having a hard time finishing. It was almost like there was this resistance I couldn't get through. Every time I looked at my computer, I couldn't get myself to finish.

Then one morning, I saw an old jar the kids made me for

Mother's Day. I opened up the jar and there were sweet handwritten notes from all the kids and when I saw Jacob's notes I just broke down in tears. I went to the backyard and cried for two hours.

While I was in the backyard crying, I got a text from a friend asking me if I was open to talking to her friend about a message she believed to be from Jacob. I agreed to talk to her.

I talked to her on the phone then she proceeded to tell me, "Jacob wants you to hurry up and finish, he wants his story to be told."

I just broke down again and knew Jacob was not going to let me slack off. He was holding me accountable even from the other side.

That evening, I stayed up until 3:00AM to finish the last round of edits. Thank you, Jacob, for giving me the strength to finish and keep going. I love you so much!

G.I.V.E. Principle

Grounding

As you breathe today, focus on the signs and wonders you might miss if you are going too fast or not paying attention. It is interesting to read about people's experiences with signs from the other side.

A friend of mine sent me a book called *Signs*. It is amazing how many signs show up when you are paying attention.

Today as you breathe, allow yourself the openness to experience signs and wonders. As you exhale, let go of doubts and fears. Let go of any preconceived notions about your belief system just for this moment.

Allow yourself to be free and open. Now continue to breathe through all five senses.

Intention: Signs and wonders

One of the challenges I hear from grieving families is that they don't feel their loved one around them anymore. It is especially challenging when they hear stories from other families who have incredible experiences of dreams, visits, and signs.

All I can say is, don't overthink it. I walk every morning and I talk to Jacob. I feel his presence. I say hello and I ask him to give me a sign.

Sometimes I'll see a heart shaped rock or leaf, a butterfly, a hummingbird, or a cloud in the sky that looks like an angel. If I over intellectualize it, it seems silly and insignificant. If I open myself up to feeling his presence, then I'm free to feel him around me.

If you find yourself reminiscing and remembering a beautiful memory during your meditation, stay present and savor the moment. Take this time to slow down and open your eyes to the possibility that your loved one is trying to get your attention.

Visualization

I love it when people send me these texts. I can just visualize Jacob and his shenanigans. Jacob was always such a prankster. I love hearing stories of how he made his friends laugh and all his crazy antics. I envision those memories and keep them close to my heart. I envision receiving more signs and wonders.

I love seeing them and hearing about them. They warm my heart.

Express Gratitude

I am so grateful for all the signs and wonders I personally get to experience, as well as the signs others get to experience and share with me.

> " I love knowing that there is still a part of Jacob around us, watching over us, guiding us.

I truly feel Jacob's presence and guidance as I finish this book. Whenever I doubt or second guess myself, Jacob is right there, encouraging me and holding me accountable to do it. Jacob was such a great example of someone who didn't just talk about what he wanted to do. He did it! He was so bold and courageous. I want to be more like him.

Jacob, even though your life was cut short, I am in awe of all the lives that you have impacted.

This book is for you and I will always love you, son. Not a moment goes by that I am not thinking about you. I am grateful for your presence during this journey, helping me, encouraging me, and telling me to keep going and not give up!

You were fearless with your dreams. Thank you for showing me how to be fearless with mine.

Beautiful Tragedy

200

Chapter 39 Nurture

"You gain strength, courage, and confidence by every experience in which you really stop to look fear in the face. You are able to say to yourself, 'I lived through this horror. I can take the next thing that comes along.'"

ELEANOR ROOSEVELT

This is my social media post today:

"Rough day today. First day back at work. Had a panic attack last night and couldn't sleep. Couldn't figure out what was happening. Last night, it overwhelmingly got real that Jacob isn't coming back. I started reeling and I couldn't calm myself down.

"I prayed and prayed and finally went to sleep. It was a restless sleep, I kept waking up. Work was great. It felt good to see my wonderful, beautiful clients. There were some that didn't know about what happened to Jacob and I had to say the words, 'My son passed away.'

"I realized I don't say that. Saying that means it's true. That was hard. The longer I don't say it out loud, the longer I prevent the inevitable. I have to keep saying it. I don't want to, but I have to. Jacob died. My one and only son died on June 27, 2019. I'll never be okay. That's okay. I will find purpose for this pain. Every day I will choose to get up and live. I love you forever, Jacob. Love, Mom

"I have my moments of grief and I just let it pass. I don't try to stop the waves from coming. I stay in it until it passes. Tears come when I am at Target for some reason. So, I push my cart and I cry, and I make everyone around me uncomfortable. I am not afraid of tears. Tears are energy, grief is energy, and you must release it.

> ❝ Grief must have a place to go or it may manifest itself through anxiety, depression, and physical ailments.

I just started therapy and my therapist is impressed at how I am coping with grief. I don't have anything to compare it to, so it was nice to get validation from a professional that I wasn't being delusional. She pointed out that I might have the characteristics of "Post Traumatic Growth."

I was intrigued and I researched it further. I thought, "Maybe I have a super-hero power and I'm different!" Well, come to find out, Post Traumatic Growth is not a special superpower, it is actually a learned skill.

There are three main characteristics of highly resilient people.

1. People who have emotional intelligence and have strong self-awareness skills are more apt to bounce back and grow through adversity.

2. People who deal with their trauma and are pro-active about their healing grow through their trauma.

3. People who are connected to a safe community and can share with others who have a shared experience, heal and are able to, in turn, help others.

I was so encouraged because I feel like this is how I have lived my life for the past fifteen years. I have been diligent about my own personal growth and dealing with my trauma. I am an advocate for helping others heal and grow. I became a Life Coach and a Grief Recovery Method Specialist® because of my personal experiences and empathy for others.

Grief has many faces. Grief can look like tears, laughter, shock, pain, joy; it is ALL of it. No judgment, no expectations, no timetable, it just is. Be okay with where you are today. It will pass, and it will come back.

During this time, make sure you nurture yourself, and allow others to pour into you.

G.I.V.E. Principle

Grounding

Today, as you inhale in resilience, strength, tenacity, and a fighter's spirit, surrender all of it and bask in the idea that your strength is in your ability to surrender.

The more you realize how NOT in control you are, the more freeing life becomes. So, breathe in and exhale out all the energy in your body that feels like it is keeping you together. Let go and let God hold you. Let God nurture you during this season of grief. Continue to breathe and connect to your five senses.

Intention: Nurture

I am a survivor and my resilience comes from years, decades, of perseverance and pushing through. I'm a tough cookie and a fighter.

When I met with my therapist, she encouraged me to be open to the idea that maybe I'm entering a new season to learn new coping skills to nurture myself.

I remember leaving her office hyper ventilating, having a panic attack as if she had just said something horrifying! The word nurture scared me because it was foreign to me.

I know how to fight, persevere, have tenacity, and survive. Nurture was not in my vocabulary.

This was my season to learn how to have self compassion, learn how to have boundaries, and learn how to honor myself. It was time to get rid of old tools of survival that no longer served me and to pick up new tools to practice self love.

Visualization

I visualize the world learning tools on how to help someone who is grieving. The best program in my opinion is the Grief Recovery Method®. I envision this method taught in schools, in counseling, in the military, in rehab centers, and every place where we can reach out to people who are grieving.

I envision this tool to be in the hands of every person in the world. I imagine a world where therapy and meditation centers are as common as having a Starbucks on every corner.

I visualize people healing and being compassionate with one another. I envision young kids, teens, and young adults learning healthy coping skills and making mental health an essential part of their lives. I visualize many people going through this book together with me and feeling a sense of connection.

My prayer is that when you read this book, you will find just a little bit of peace and be reminded that you are not alone. I hope every person reading my story finds healing and a safe community of nonjudgmental people to walk alongside them through their journey.

I visualize giving you, the reader, a big hug. I visualize sitting with you as we try to navigate our new normal together. I also envision grievers reading my family's story and feeling empowered to live, create, and manifest the dreams that are still in your heart. Our loved ones may have died, but we can still be fully alive. Alive for them. Let's carry the torch, my friends. I love you.

Express Gratitude

I am so grateful to be in a healthy community in Arizona. I am grateful we are in a season where we can take time to heal. We are giving ourselves a lot of grace and we are allowing others to nurture us during this difficult season. I am so grateful for our CCV (Christ Church of the Valley) family and staff for the way they have taken such good care of us. I am grateful for my Body Lab family, clients and co-workers, and how they have rallied behind me and given me a place to work and continue to do what I love to do.

I am grateful to my therapist who has been a safe person and given me great tools to heal.

I'm grateful for my online community that Vicki and I lead and how we are all transforming and healing together. Thank you.

Chapter 40 Connection

"I define connection as the energy that exists between people when they feel seen, heard, and valued; when they can give and receive without judgment; and when they derive sustenance and strength from the relationship."

BRENÉ BROWN

" " We are created for community and connection. We are not meant to live this life alone.

I am overwhelmed with gratitude for the support I have been given. I have gotten so many messages from people I have never met and will never meet, and they share their love for Jacob. I love the stories they share about how Jacob impacted their life. I am so inspired by my son's ability to connect with so many hurting people even though he was going through deep despair.

He was a light. A bright light dimmed too soon. I am overcome with joy by the way young people, friends and fans reach out to me with their hearts so open and vulnerable.

Here are a few messages we have received about how Jacob impacted them:

- "Jacob 'Hella Sketchy' has been the biggest producer/artist inspiration to me. I connected to his energy and how he expressed it in his art. His hard work, starting at a young age, really struck me. I am going through a dark time and his music gets me through it."

- "Hello, I got your number from Jacob's memorial. I didn't know Jacob personally, but his music did stop me from committing suicide and through his death, I have stopped using drugs. Prayers and have a blessed day."

- "Thank you for being great parents to Sketchy. We are all so grateful to have you guys connect with us and have a community for us. I don't have anyone to talk to about my problems. Thank you for listening."

- "Jacob changed my life and so many other people."

- "I am so sorry for your loss. I don't have a mom and I am on my own. Music has been my safe place and Jacob's music was a big part of my life and still is. Thank you."

- "Your son helped me and was an amazing person who showed love to his fans, he inspired a lot of people."

- "How did Jacob do his hair? Oh, and RIP by the way!"

Are there people in your community you want to connect with? Whether it is school, church, workplace, or a club of some sort, consider getting involved.

Healing happens within a community and it is done through safe, honest conversations. They are out there, I promise. If you can't find one, connect with me online and I will add you to our online community.

I cannot imagine what I would do without community. The level of support we have received is humbling. There are no words. Thank you is not sufficient.

I want to pay it forward and find ways to love all who are hurting.

G.I.V.E. Principle

Grounding

It is time to connect to your breath. Make sure your back is supported. Inhale new breath, new air, new energy. Exhale out everything you don't need.

With every inhale, focus on connecting to every part of your body. Evaluate this: how are you showing up for yourself?

Focus on being your own safe place. Remember that we cannot give what we do not have.

Intention: Connection

> "Teacher, which is the greatest commandment in the Law?" Jesus replied: " 'Love the Lord your God with all your heart and with all your soul and with all your mind.' This is the first and greatest commandment. And the second is like it: 'Love your neighbor as yourself.'" --Matthew 22:36-39 NIV

If you are a believer, you've heard this scripture many times. How many times have you heard a sermon about loving God? Many times, right? What about loving your neighbor? Often.

I have never heard a sermon on loving yourself. On the contrary, we are taught that thinking about yourself is selfish and vain. That's not what I'm talking about. I'm talking about having a healthy relationship with yourself. Do the work, get therapy, heal the parts of you that have been wounded and hurt.

I truly believe that lack of connection is rooted in lack of self-love. We cannot give what we do not have. Our love must come from our overflow.

In my coaching practice, I encourage people to connect to God or whatever higher power you believe in. We have to realize that in order to get through these tough times, it's going to take power greater than ourselves.

Once you connect to God, you need to connect with yourself. These tools are just that. This meditation practice is a form of self love and replenishes the soul. Self care is a form of self love and should not be neglected. (Go to my website to get more information about specific meditations for self love.)

Lastly, we need connection with others. Healing happens in a shared community of like-minded safe people. I have learned that being authentic about my healing journey has helped others find healing as well.

I woke up from a dream and God said, "I am healing you so you can heal others!"

Healing happens when we have a witness, when we are seen, when we find a safe place to be our authentic self. I'm so grateful for my people who love me...all of me...without judgment and expectation.

We are healing together as we witness each other dealing with our stuff. Life is not easy, and life is not fair, but you can still enjoy the journey.

Visualization

I visualize everyone in this world as being part of a healthy community. A world where regardless of our differences and beliefs, we can be good humans who take care of one another. I envision a community of like-minded people serving and caring for one another. I visualize people truly being there for one another, without judgment or an agenda. I imagine a world where we are there to support each other's victories and successes.

I love that Jacob looked at the world this way. I am devastated that once he moved to L.A., he soon realized that people did not share the same convictions as he did. His gratitude and support for others left him vulnerable; he was hurt too many times, but he continued to love anyway.

Express Gratitude

I am grateful that my vision of community is not far off from my reality. It is so important to plug in to community. I am grateful for our church family, our work family, our immediate family, our dance family, Jacob's music family, our family from L.A., Texas, Arizona, and the Philippines. I am so grateful for our online family and people all over the world who have supported us.

If you feel alone and isolated, I promise you, you are not alone. Connect with us, we will welcome you with open arms. We love you!

CONCLUSION
What You Need Is Inside Of You

"Everything in the universe is within you.
Ask all from yourself."

RUMI

I cannot believe this is our last day together. If you made it this far, THANK YOU! Thank you for walking alongside as I process my grief journey with you. In times of grief, it is easy to feel like you are never going to get over it. I want to remind you that you have survived so much in your life up to this point.

You have everything you need already inside of you.

> Every time you lived by faith, you put that trust in your faith tank. Every time you persevered, you put that experience in your resilience tank. Every time you overcame adversity, you added that to your list of victories.

I want to remind you of how strong you are. What you sow, you will reap. We often hear this said in regard to what we are giving to those around us, but what are you pouring into your own soul? What you pour in will grow. Be sure to pour in a good dose of patience and gentleness and it will be there when you need it.

Our tears are a deposit and we put them in the reservoir of our resilience. We need resilience to survive this life. Our pain will give us strength if we allow it to propel us into positive action.

It is in you. What you do every day creates the outcome for your future. The little things we do prepare us for the big things! What you do in private will be exposed in public!

Wholehearted living, to me, means being authentic. I am pretty much an open book if you haven't figured that out already. I may be a lot of things, but fake isn't one of them. I always have to get everything off my chest, even if it makes others uncomfortable.

Living transparently and authentically is so freeing. Consider what your life would look like if you did. I choose to live this way because, for me, there is so much freedom in it.

You see, I don't ever have to worry about people finding out I have skeletons in my closet. As a matter a fact, I will freely give you a tour and introduce you to all my skeletons. I have nothing to fear, I do not have to hide in darkness. That my friends, is freedom. That is wholehearted living!

The more I shine the light in my life to reveal hidden corners, the more freedom it brings. Rather than being judged, which is typically why we don't share, I have found that it helps others to not feel isolated and alone.

On this journey of grief, I have chosen to be very vocal and open about our journey of addiction, mental illness, spiritual oppression, and other deep-seeded, silent challenges. I am not sure where God is taking it, but I commit my steps to Him daily and I choose to obey the direction He wants me to go.

Maybe you are reading this book because you are a parent and you want to be proactive and aware of how to navigate these delicate years. Maybe you have kids Jacob's age and you can't imagine how you would process a tragedy like this. Maybe you have a loved one who is struggling with substance abuse or mental illness.

Sadly, there are way too many people struggling and we cannot pretend it isn't an issue or think that we can wish it away or just pray it away. We must take action and be part of the solution.

What does that look like? Check our resource guide and connect with our community. We will continue to equip and empower you to move forward.

I am so grateful for the opportunity to encourage you. I truly believe you don't give yourself enough credit. What you need is already inside of you. Your strength, resilience, faith, hope, love, it's in there. I don't care who you are or what you've done. You are created in God's image. You have the ability to change and grow. All you need is to take one step in the right direction.

We all have choices. Choose to live your life in total surrender and trust that if you move toward growth, you will find life after tragedy.

It will still hurt, and it won't be easy, but I promise you if you keep showing up and moving forward you will get stronger. I am so grateful you are reading this book. I love you. I am here for you. I believe in you. You matter. Your story matters. You are needed in this world. The world needs what you have to give.

How To Support Your Grieving Friend

Show up for your grieving friend. Even as I write this, I have had a couple of friends lose their loved ones. I am definitely a little more sensitive to what they may be feeling. I sent a gift and a note of encouragement to my friend out of town and I made dinner for my local friend.

Not only does serving others encourage them, it also encourages me to be able to bless people around me. It helps me put my energy and attention on something other than my own grief. Here are some helpful pointers:

Please be a good listener and avoid statements like:

- "He/she is in a better place."
- "At least you had them for (fill in blank)…
- "Don't be sad."
- "Just move on!"
- "Be grateful you had (fill in blank)…
- "You should…"
- "Time heals all wounds."
- "I know how you feel."

These are well-meaning, but *not* helpful statements.

Instead, say things like:

- "What happened? I'm here for you."
- "I am so sorry. I am here to listen."
- "I am praying for you." (And really pray for them)

Validate what your friend is feeling:

- "I am sorry you feel that way."
- "I can't imagine what you're going through."
- "I miss him/her, too."

Try to anticipate what your friend might need, instead of asking, "What do you need? What can I do for you?"

[Honestly, when someone is grieving, they might not know what they need].

Instead, be proactive. Here are some helpful ideas:

- Set up meals.
- Clean their house.
- Set up childcare or pet care.
- Take them out for self-care, massages, nails, hair, short hikes or walks.
- Cards, notes, and all forms of well wishes really go a long way.
- Chocolates and ice cream are always welcome too; and stay and eat it with them.

It is normal and tempting to think your grieving friend needs space, but in actuality what they really need is another human to share their grief. You might feel awkward and uncomfortable, it is okay. Push through and show up for your friend.

Grieving doesn't just include death. It can be divorce, a big move, change in careers, big life change, illness, and other events that temporarily stop us in our tracks.

Remember, one of the definitions of grief is "Conflicting emotions due to the end of a familiar pattern or behavior."

So in a sense, we are all grieving.

Honestly, the best thing you can do is to be by their side, listen, and hold a safe place for them with no agenda. You are not there to fix them.

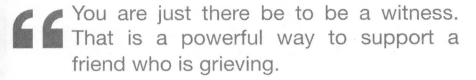

> You are just there be to be a witness. That is a powerful way to support a friend who is grieving.

The support and love that we are able to receive is in direct proportion to the openness and vulnerability of expressing what we need. Let me say that again. If you don't ever ask for help, you won't get it. If you don't ever show your weakness, you won't be surrounded by strength!!!

We are ALL going to go through seasons where we need people. It is okay to need help.

I am grateful I was introduced to the Grief Recovery Method® over fifteen years ago. I know for a fact it has helped me get through so much grief and heartache. It is essential to my healing process. It is helping me mend my broken heart as we speak.

I am determined to help people and be part of the solution.

Acknowledgments

Thank you to my girlfriends who I walk with daily and share my good, bad, and ugly. Vicki Hagadorn, Robin Noll, and Sandi Derby are my ride or die friends. They know me and they still love me. I love you guys so much! I don't know where I would be without you.

Thank you to Erin Macleod who helped with my book edit early in the infant stages of my story. Thank you for being a faithful friend. I love you.

Thank you to Kelleigh Averill whose voice I trusted to edit and see the book through the lens of the person needing the support and encouragement. You are a gem and not only am I grateful for your incredible editing and communication skills, I love having you as a friend.

To Annie Preston, my final editor that God brought to my life for many reasons. Thank you for making this happen.

Thank you to Daniel Hagadorn for your patience and care with formatting, editing, and formatting again. I couldn't have done this without you.

Thank you to my book coach and mentor, Christine Gail, and the Unleash Your Rising community. Thank you for your kindness and support every step of the way!

Thank you to our CCV Community in Arizona who continues to pour out encouragement, support, safety, and security when we need it most. Your generosity will never be forgotten.

Thank you for valuing Erik and allowing him to have flexibility and time off during our time of grief. Your leadership team has taken such great care of our family. Words cannot express our gratitude.

Thank you to Mosaic in Hollywood. We believe in what you are doing and how you are reaching the creative community in Hollywood and beyond. We are with you and will never forget the kindness and generosity you showed us in our deepest darkness.

Thank you to Pastor Erwin McManus for hosting and officiating the memorial for Jacob. Your encouraging words will forever impact our hearts and all who listen. Thank you for being a faith leader in Jacob's life. Your sermon was the last one he ever heard. Our last family outing was at Mosaic. That will be a lasting memory for our family. Thank you!

Thank you, Steve and Jackie Morici, for being such faithful friends. Thank you for coming to the hospital, feeding us, loving us, and praying for us. Steve, thank you for officiating Jacob's funeral. We will never forget your kindness and generosity.

Thank you to Michelle Julian for creating a Go Fund Me for our family and taking such good care of us. We love you so much.

Thank you to Gina Alexander for helping us with the memorial and being such an awesome friend.

Thank you to our Austin Texas family and all who attended the memorial. We love you and cherished our time there.

Thank you to Chris and Irma Torres, Mike and Kim Upton, Andrea Burns, Karen Garces, Katie Rivezzo, Lori Mamby, Gina Marchant, Jesse, Keyawna, Jackie, Kel, Hannah, Bobby, Gica Malbas, Izzy, Vanessa Garcia, Gina and Rich Alexander, Katie and Makenna, Akira, Kayode, Ade, the Agbalaya Family,

Ghostrage, Bambi, Mason Flynt, Chris Baello, Keagan Hoffman, Thor Putnam, Justin Shiro, Joe, Diablo, Sauve, Curtis, D1, Midnight Society, Bandkids, GBC, Wiggy, Aaron, Tyler, Jesus Honcho, Ezra, Dogceo, Garzi, Chandler, Austin, Jamaal, The Speaks family, Charlie Shuffler, Eyekeem, Maestro, KK, JD, Kamiyada, Andrew, The Thure's, Matt and Jill Dickens, Richard and Ricky Ransier, Lyle and Langston, Nicole Hogan, Esther and Abe Willows, Susan Agostenelli, Angie Nakamoto, Shelly Jones, Katrina Gibson, Joe and Pandora, Eddie Boy and family, and everyone else who came to visit us at the hospital. Your time, your encouragement, your prayers were so needed, and we will never forget you. Sorry if I didn't write your name down, there were so many of you. You know who you are. We love you!

Lil Tecca, Lil Mosey, Juice Wrld, Lil Peep, Green Day, and Pierce the Veil, for making Jacob happy with your music.

Thank you to Mike Caren, Jeff Vaughn, Eli Piccarreta and everyone else from Atlantic Records for believing in my son and giving him a platform. Thank you for your generosity and kindness. We will never forget you and what you did for Jacob.

Simon, Jacob's AA Sponsor. Thank you for trying.

Thank you to my counselor, Jen Cecil. You are a gift!

Thank you to Glenn Marsden of the Imperfectly Perfect Campaign. Let's do this!!!

Thank you to Eden and Kim of Talk, Purpose, and Truth podcast for creating a platform for people to share their authentic self.

Kim & Michelle Humphrey and everyone at Parents of Addicted Loved Ones (PAL), thank you for your support and all the great work you are doing to support parents.

To Mindie, Alon, and Haley, thank you for opening up your home and letting us have our private resort to grieve and get away. We love you guys!

To Tani, thank you for being by Jacob's side and being such an awesome cousin to Jacob. You were such a rock for us during this tragic time. We love you.

To the doctors, nurses, and staff at Hollywood Presbyterian, THANK YOU! We know you guys tried your best. We are s grateful for the way you took such great care of Jacob. We felt your love and compassion. To Nurse Jamie, you were an ange and we will never forget how you grieved with us as if Jacob was your own little brother.

Thank you to the countless fans, friends, acquaintances, family members, online friends who supported us and continue to support us, whether financially, with words of encouragement, and just sharing with us what Jacob meant to you. We are eternally grateful.

To Zeny Salgado (Granma Sketchy) Thank you for being Jacob's cool, hip Granma. He loved you so much.

To the Wilcher's, there are no words for the encouragement and support you gave us during this challenging time. We love you so much!

To Rory, Susan, Carlos, and the rest of the family. We love you and we're so grateful for you and the time we shared.

To Amy Ram, thank you for visiting and grieving with me. You were one of the first families I ever met that dealt with addiction and I watched your strength and grace as you dealt with the challenges in your own family. Thank you for taking care of my family.

To John and Karen, thank you for being Jacob's surrogate parents while he navigated his time on his own in Hollywood making his record. I know he gave you guys gray hair and aged you just like he did with us! We love the way you took him in like your very own son. I know he loved you guys and was grateful for the opportunity.

To Evelyn, thank you for being Jacob's girlfriend and being a true friend to him when he needed it most. You are every mother's dream girlfriend. The way you cared for Jacob and the way you never left his side is admirable and we will never forget it. I am so happy to have you as part of our family now. We are here for you forever and always.

To Erik, my baby daddy. You are the GOAT! Whenever I stalked Jacob on his social media, (I made fake accounts and stalked him and all his friends) Sorry, not sorry...it would warm my heart to hear Jacob say that his dad was the GOAT! (Greatest Of All Time) Jacob was so proud of you and so am I. I love you so much and I thank you for pushing me and believing in me, and making me write a road map, and ticking me off at times, and constantly being my best friend. I love you and I couldn't do this without you.

To Emma, my favorite middle child. You amaze me. Your level of maturity and strength was the glue that kept us together during our dark time. I love you so much and I believe in you. You are already so incredibly successful because you are fearless, and you are so smart. I love traveling the world with you. I love just hanging out with you. You are my rock. I love you.

To Sydney, my baby. I remember the days right after Jacob died and I felt so guilty for being paralyzed by grief. I would just cry, and you would say, "Don't cry mom, Jacob wouldn't want you to be sad."

You are right. You inherited Jacob's fun spirit. You can always make us laugh and smile, even through the most challenging times. I love you so much and I am so proud of you. Just please stop tickling me.

To Jacob…

What can I say!? I really feel like you propelled this book and my purpose to another level. You took every last fear and insecurity out of my heart and made me "pee or get off the pot!"

You taught me so much in your eighteen years here on Earth. You taught me how to give my whole heart and not care what anyone thinks. You taught me to be authentic and say everything I need to say without holding back. You taught me to be more compassionate and empathetic as I have learned from your friends and fans.

You truly were too good for this world. I am grateful I had you for a little while. Truly not enough time, but I know you're trolling us and enjoying every minute of it.

I love you forever, I love you for always, as long as I am living, my baby you will be.

Resources

Parents of Addicted Loved Ones (PAL)

Part of the proceeds of this book will go to support PAL. We have chosen to invest in PAL because they do an incredible job empowering, strengthening, and equipping parents on how to navigate this new normal.

Erik and I found PAL in April of 2019. I wish we would have found PAL sooner. Our son was struggling with substance abuse. The last two years were spent on doctors, rehabs, ER visits, AA, NA, you name it! We did it all!

What we didn't realize was as parents, we needed support as well. We found that support at PAL. It was so eye-opening to be around other families battling this nightmare.

The teaching and training at PAL gave us tools and strength to fight the battle ahead of us. We will continue to share information about PAL because it is an important resource for families.

We are so thankful for the support we have been given. Please look for a PAL group near you if you have a loved one struggling with addiction.

www.palgroup.org or call **602-512-1454.**

The Grief Recovery Method®

I have been using the Grief Recovery tools for the last decade. All my best friends are Grief Specialists, so I was surrounded by the best during this tragedy.

It occurred to me that all losses are not the same. Losing someone to a drug overdose brings so much shame and stigma. Families that are dealing with substance abuse, addiction, mental illness, and suicides, are not only suffering greatly, but they are suffering in silence and in isolation.

As a parent of a child who overdosed, it is natural to feel an enormous amount of guilt. Woulda-shoulda-coulda invade your thoughts.

I had thoughts like, 'If only we kept him in athletics, he wouldn't be struggling, or if only we put him in regular school and not homeschooled him, or if only we made him more committed to go to church and bible studies with us, if we just loved him more, if…if…the thoughts continue.

When we went to rehab, I remember sitting in a session with all the other families. One kid had to forfeit his full ride academic scholarship due to his addiction, another forfeited his athletic scholarship, another was a part of a super devout religious family and the parents couldn't understand where they went wrong, another kid had a single mom who loved her son so much that it was clear love alone couldn't save him.

The families represented in that room showed me that addiction does not discriminate. Mental illness does not discriminate.

 Families are living in so much shame because we blame ourselves.

Recently I read about a pastor and a public figure on social media who was an advocate for mental illness and people who struggled with suicidal thoughts. I followed him for his authentic, inspirational posts. I often prayed that Jacob would find a Christian support system to help him navigate his new life in Hollywood.

To my dismay, this young man, despite his role as a pastor, and advocate for mental illness, and who was surrounded by his beautiful family and friends still succumbed to suicide. It makes me want to lose hope...but I do not have that luxury.

There are too many people out there who need just that: hope.

I am going to do my part to be a "hope dealer." I want to bring hope to families and individuals with my grief coaching. I completed my certification so I can share these life-giving tools to as many people as possible.

I will be hosting live classes in Phoenix, Arizona, and online. I also host retreat getaways to connect with like-minded individuals and create a space for deep healing.

The tools I learned from Grief Recovery are priceless. I am so grateful I had these tools through this challenging season. If I am going to be completely honest, I feel like Jacob's physical death was the second death.

We found ourselves grieving Jacob when we found out he was struggling with substance abuse issues. It was so hard to face the fact that I was grieving lost hopes, dreams, and expectations. To grieve someone while they are still alive is grueling.

One of the definitions of grief is, "An end to a familiar pattern or behavior."

I had to come to grips that life as we knew it would not be the same.

Because of these tools, I was able to be fully present with my son. The last few years, I was able to share everything in my heart and I left nothing unsaid. I was able to let my son go with peace in my heart that Jacob undeniably knew he was loved and that we would do anything for him.

www.griefrecoverymethod.com

BUILDING COMMUNITY

It is my desire to see you get plugged in to a healthy, safe community. If you don't know where to go, here are some options where you are always welcome...

Get Inspired Movement

We have a closed Facebook community group to encourage, equip, and empower you to live your best life. Join like-minded individuals as we share tools and encouragement to help equip you to grow. We all need community and this a safe, non-judgmental group to rally around you.

Find us on Facebook **@Get Inspired Movement**.

Self Care...Soul Care

Along with Vicki Hagadorn, we facilitate a 28-Day mastermind group to walk alongside your healing journey. We offer this program seasonally.

Find us at **www.selfcaresoulcaremastermind.com**

Journey to Wholeness

Join my friends and me on a holistic wellness retreat to re-charge, re-boot, and re-invent yourself.

Find us on **www.judythureson.com**

Helping Parents Heal

A non-profit organization dedicated to assisting bereaved parents, giving them support and resources to aid in the healing process.

www.helpingparentsheal.org and on Facebook

Keynote, Workshop, Event, or Training Leader
How to Rise Up in the Midst of Pain!

If you are looking for a speaker to help inspire your organization, employees, community, school, or faith group then consider inviting Judy Thureson to your next event.

Judy has the ability to inspire and motivate people, not just with her inspirational stories of resilience and tenacity but with her proven strategies and actionable steps that lead to hope and healing.

Judy's message is a universal message of how to rise from the ashes and build a powerful story in the midst of pain and suffering. Judy will equip, empower, and encourage you to take the next step on your journey.

Judy will customize a program that will meet your needs. She is available for consulting and leading breakthrough strategy workshops to help your organization achieve your goals.

For more information about Judy Thureson:

www.judythureson.com

Follow Judy on social media:

F facebook.com/beautifultragedybook

I @judythureson

L judythureson

Speaking, coaching, and media inquiries:

www.judythureson.com | judy@judythureson.com

ABOUT THE AUTHOR

Judy Thureson is an author, speaker, and transformation coach. Her desire to see people live their most authentic life has helped hundreds of clients over the last decade get results by focusing on their mental, physical, and spiritual health.

Judy has numerous certifications in health and wellness, leads retreats, workshops, conferences, and offers online coaching to equip and educate people about the importance of holistic wellness, including those suffering from grief and loss.

In Austin, Texas she co-founded Get Inspired Movement, a women's empowerment group with her best friend Vicki and continues to equip women online.

She lives in Arizona with her husband Erik, and their daughters, Emma and Sydney. You can find her doing yoga, enjoying the outdoors, eating tacos, playing with her dog Angel, writing, hiking, and loving Jesus!

Made in the USA
San Bernardino, CA
23 July 2020